The Unknotting
Identifying the Roots of Dysfunction

KIKA ASHANIKE

Copyright © 2017 Kika Ashanike

All rights reserved. Except as permitted under UK copyright, Designs and Patent Act 1988, no part of this publication may be reproduced, distributed, or transmitted in any form or by any means, or stored in a database or retrieval system, without prior written permission of the publisher.

Unless otherwise noted, Scripture quotations are from the King James Version of the Holy Bible. Public Domain

Scripture quotations marked (NIV) are taken from the Holy Bible, New International Version®, NIV®. Copyright © 1973, 1978, 1984, 2011 by Biblica, Inc.™ Used by permission of Zondervan. All rights reserved worldwide. www.zondervan.com

States Scripture quotations marked (AMP) are taken from the Amplified Bible, Copyright © 1954, 1958, 1962, 1964, 1965, 1987 by The Lockman Foundation. Used by permission.

Cover design: 40k design

Interior formatting: Pura Track

LoveChild Publishing
A trading name of LoveChild Trust
London, United Kingdom
First edition: August 2017
ISBN 978-1-5272-1285-5

DEDICATION

To every family that has ever walked through brokenness, and for every child that is the product of brokenness; trust and believe that our God gives beauty for ashes, He can mend the most fractured of units and breathe life into dead situations. New legacies can be created when you give yourself over to His Unknotting.

ACKNOWLEDGMENTS

Mum, I'm certain that no other woman on this planet could have mothered me the way you have. I am assured that the Lord handpicked you to carefully cradle this destiny and guide me into the woman that I am today. Thank you for always supporting the call on my life and encouraging me. Thank you for every Nando's run as I sat in my room and obeyed the Lord's call for me to write.

Seyi, you are the dream that sisters are made of! You came into my life at a time when I needed a helping hand the most, thank you for unselfishly always saying yes to support me.

Torema, the sister that models what chasing after the Father looks like and the sister that I have no doubt, will show the world what basking in the promise land after enduring adversity *feels* like. You are seen and you are loved! Thank you for being an example without ever uttering a word.

Aunty Sumbo, your strength, your refusal to quit, your love and your care is next to none. I love and appreciate you. Keep putting one foot in front of the other, one day at a time, you'll soon look up and see greenery, peace and favour all around you.

Edrick, you are the mentor of mentors! Thank you for being a father and a friend. Thank you for every rebuke, though I hated them, I needed them. Thank you for caring not about my feelings, but about my destiny.

Pure Hearts ladies, for every retreat attendee, every conference guest and more, for every conference I have ever been invited to speak at, every person I've ever prayed for and with. Thank you for being true examples that have helped me to put together this book. What a gift to steward, I'm thankful!

CONTENTS

Pre-Introduction   xi
Introduction   13

SECTION 1: IDENTIFYING ROOTS
Chapter 1: Family under siege   27
Chapter 2: Children of failed marriages   35
Chapter 3: Paternal ties   49
Chapter 4: Maternal ties   65

SECTION 2: EFFECTS OF DYSFUNCTION
Chapter 5: Knots, marriages & families   77
Chapter 6: dysfunctional behaviours   87

SECTION 3: FINDING FREEDOM
Chapter 7: The root of rejection   105
Chapter 8: Pilgrim of memories   123
Chapter 9: The curse of King Jeconiah   139
Chapter 10: Creating new legacies   159

Unknotting trees   171
Notes   174

PRE-INTRODUCTION

Who is this book for?

This book is for the one with questions. It is for those looking for their soul's freedom. It provides answers for the child that grew up without their father, estranged from their mother, in a loveless home or the contrary. It brings clarity for the one that grew up afraid or feels robbed of parts of their childhood. It traces back the steps and encourages an analysis into the family structure. It is in essence a book fo all, it is pages full of answers.

In this book, you may find that that which you have identified as your norm is in no way normal at all. You will learn to call dysfunction just that; dysfunctional. You will learn to identify issues and personality traits that have acted as weeds on the bed of your life, emotions or mind. You will see very clearly that no tree just grows bad fruit. There is a root and a source to every life issue. Unfortunately, most of these roots are often found in the breakdown or malfunctioning of the family unit.

There is no breaking free, there is a setting free

Before tackling the Unknotting, one thing to keep in mind are the words of Jesus in John 8:36:

> *"If the Son therefore shall set you free,
> ye shall be free indeed".*

It is paramount that we understand that there is no such thing as self-freedom. We can't read our way or study our way to freedom, it is the Son alone who sets free. The second thing that I have come to learn is that it is indeed a setting free and not a breaking free that the Lord does in us. If He is to set us free then we must be patient whilst that process of freedom takes place. We must endure and stand whilst the Lord Himself takes us through.

INTRODUCTION

What does it mean to be knotted?

Recently the Lord began to show me that the world was full of knotted people. Individuals have been so hurt and damaged by their family structure, their upbringing or generational patterns, that though often unaware, they have resorted to attempting to live the best dysfunctional life on offer. 'Dysfunctional' in and of itself simply meaning, *"not operating normally or properly"*.

The truth is that the earth is full of tied up men and women. Men and women that are tied up in their emotions, tied up in their minds, tied up in their thinking and entangled in the knots of their past. Being no respecter of persons, dysfunction takes no prisoners nor does it favour a particular people group. Men and women with great jobs are tied up, men and women working for the Lord are tied up, tied up political figures are running our country, raising our children, teaching them in classrooms, treating us at hospitals and begging us for money on the streets. The attack on the family unit has produced a world full of those with knotted souls.

What are knots?

I refer to dysfunction as knots for one simple reason. When the Lord began to take me through my own process of the unknotting I felt as though He was gently unravelling me from dysfunction that had *entangled* me overtime. Knots begin to take place in one's life when the initial dysfunction within a family occurs. When a child is released by the Lord into a family, it is functional and in God's order for the child to firstly be placed into a home that contains both a biological mother and a biological father. With statistics of single parent homes on the rise and children being given up for adoption (adoption in of itself being an incredible act of love mirroring the grace of Heaven); however, for the child that has been given up for adoption, we cannot deny that the spirit of rejection and abandonment crouches at the door of such a soul. For many of us therefore, the first major knot (dysfunction if you like) in our life is already created before we even enter into the earth. For some of us, knots are created in our soul even in our foetal stage when our unwanted pregnancy and our coming into the world was perceived an obstacle rather than a blessing. We may have been the product of an affair, a one-night stand, an unwanted pregnancy or in more sinister cases, rape or abuse. It is functional for a child to be released by the Lord through a consenting married mother and father. It is again functional for a child to be released by the Lord into a home that is full of true love and peace, a marriage joined together by the Lord and not by man, to have a child born into a home lacking these vital surroundings is to subject a child to knots in their soul *before* they are even born.

    I remember when the Lord began to highlight this to me and puzzled I said to Him, *"but Lord not having a Father growing up didn't affect me, I had an incredible mother and we surely didn't want for anything"*. What I failed to realise was that whilst my physical needs were being met, my soul was thirsting. Knot after knot was being created in my personality, my way of thinking and my perception of my self-worth and value were diminishing. The Lord responded to me, *"Getting used to dysfunction so much so that it **feels** like normality is much worse than the one obviously affected by the dysfunction"*. You see for me, I had grown used to dysfunction because it was all that I had ever known. It was like having a table on 3 legs and the table proclaims its soundness and perfect use. Though the table may have grown accustomed to standing aided on 3 legs, it was never created to hobble along but to stand majestically. It was created to have its weight spread evenly across four legs just as you and I were created to be born into an atmosphere that contained a biological mother, father, a home full of love, containing whole, healed and emotionally well balanced and sound parents with complete identities in Christ Jesus. To have anything *other* than this is to be born *outside* of God's (and not man's) functioning normal, it is to be born into dysfunction. Yes, surely God can and does use dysfunction for His glory, I stand a living witness to this. In fact, I believe He delights in opportunities for such to display His power. We have witnessed Him grace families to raise successful children in the 21st century and seen single parent homes produce some of the world's first-class students; however, these children (I refrain from saying all, but certainly many), when examined and searched, grow up to display scars in their personalities and ways of thinking, indicative of a dysfunctional foundation.

Much of the inhabitants of our world are born into a lack of normalcy and very much of us have become accustomed to living wounded. You see, I believe that the greatest of Satan's attacks are the ones that look nothing like an attack at all, they are the ones that fit so beautifully into our world's new norms. The enemy has done an outstandingly wicked and crafty job at creating a world full of knotted people, a world complete with functioning dysfunction. It is my hope that through this book the Lord would highlight areas of dysfunction and knots in your soul, that He would reveal the roots, the patterns of knotting from your past or ancestry and how they are currently affecting you in your life today (your singleness, your marriage, your parenting, your relationships, finances and career, your mind, emotions and your physical body), and lastly, that through the power of prayer and the counsel of the spirit of God, you would begin to experience *The Unknotting*.

Before we begin what, I liken to the diagnosis of self, I'd like to walk you through some key subject matters that are poignant to understand before delving into the chapters of this book.

Psychology and dysfunction

In preparation for this book I went on a journey of extensive study to see what psychologists have to say about the importance of the foundational years in a child's life. I believe that much of the issues that you are dealing with, the anxiety, the married man with lust in his heart, the mother unable to fully love her own child, the jealous wife, the depression or bipolar, the emotionally imbalanced, the depressed pastor and the suicidal teen can all be traced back to the first 7 to 10 years of our lives. I am a firm believer in God's order and the biblical standards of a family home; not simply because I am a Christian, but because His way has proven to be the only way that works. The world can and continues to find 21st century modern versions to the family, it claims that daddy and daddy can raise a son, but even psychology and medical experts will vouch for the only functioning normal, being that which our God has ordained from the foundations of the world, and that is a home where one man and one woman both whole in their emotions and mind raise and nurture a sound child that can then go on to marry another sound and whole individual birthing generations of whole people. Anything constructed outside of this is to create what we have in our world today, a world full of broken individuals.

Professor of sociology, David Popenoe Phd (Rutgers University), states in an article for parenthood in America the following:

> *"Everything we know about human behaviour suggests that the family is the institution in which most children learn about character and morality. The schools, the churches, and the law can all help in the process of character development, but they have much less independent force of their own. Their main function is to reinforce what has already been taught in the home. If morality and*

character are not taught in the home, other institutions cannot be relied on to undo the damage. That is why the quality of family life is so important, and why the family is society's most fundamental institution." [1]

This of course leads one to wonder, what level of dysfunction takes place in one's soul when the family unit fails in its role? Psychologists in the American Psychological Association write that, *"wherever there is a problem child, there is a problem marriage" (Framo, 1975).*

How much do you know about the marriage of your parents? How clued up are you about the very foundation of your existence, what do you know about your conception, were you the product of a passionate night of love between a married man and woman or were you born to the mistress or lady in waiting. I heard the story of a man whose mother was told to "abort the baby" by his father, after decades of suffering from rejection he inquired of the Lord and was given the revelation that the spirit of rejection attached itself to him in the womb once his father made that statement. As hard hitting as this seems and as distressing as it may be for one to go down memory lane, to find the courage to pray through such questions that risk pain or

---

[1] http://parenthood.library.wisc.edu/Popenoe/Popenoe-Modeling.html

heartache is to discover a life of the unknotting. To be aware of one's foundation and where you come from is as key as knowing where you are going. Why do you think children who are adopted by the most cosy and stable of families always end up on a hunt for their birth families no matter how dysfunctional they suspect them to be? There is a longing in every human soul to know exactly where we come from. There are parts of your identity that will never make sense or click into place until you know of the man and woman that created you and the circumstances under which you came to be. Now of course, I don't suggest interrogating your parents as to the exact details surrounding your conception, but I do encourage slight probing into the circumstances that you were born into. Were they married? Were they happy? Were they estranged?

Now guaranteed for some of us this may be a task deemed impossible for whatever reason, but as believers in the Lord Jesus Christ, we must strongly believe in the power of the Lord to bring clarity, to bring peace, to piece together puzzles that seem impossible to fix in our own eyes.

Salvation and the unknotting

I'll deal with a question that I too asked myself as I began to write this book: *"But the blood of Jesus covers it all, when we are saved old things are passed away and the new has come, right? Why must one go back to begin the process of untying themselves from the knots of their past if Calvary covered it all?"* I wish that were the case, I truly do. However, looking at the level of dysfunction plaguing the lives of the most faithful of believers, I believe it'd be accurate to say there is a deeper work to be done even following our altar call.

The word salvation

The word salvation takes its root from the Greek word 'sozo', meaning wholeness. You see many of us seek to be saved but many of us fail to seek wholeness. I'd like to remind us of the words of Philippians 2:12 which encourages us to *"work out your own salvation with fear and trembling"*. If salvation translates to wholeness, then we can take this verse to be "work out your own wholeness with fear and trembling". It is my belief that seeking wholeness and not simply stopping at an altar call is a mandate for every Christian. I believe wholeheartedly that it is the Lord's desire to have a whole and well-balanced bride. A bride without anxiety or panic attacks, a bride not in the prayer closet one day and battling pornography desires the next, a bride without the spot of shame or the wrinkle of low self-esteem and identity

> *Many of us seek to be saved but many of us fail to seek wholeness.*

confusion, He seeks a whole bride. He wants you unknotted, He wants you free, He wants you whole.

What was saved at Calvary?

We know that man is made up of three parts just like our triune God, we are spirit, soul and body. Our body is the physical part of us that people see, our spirit is what the Lord saved when we uttered the prayer of salvation, our soul however, made up of our mind, will and emotions, is where the scars and imprints of pain and trauma from our past lie. Now unfortunately, for the majority of us, these prints, scars and dents do not disappear with a single prayer at the altar. They are painful memories that unravel and become healed as we continue on our walk with the Lord. We bring each scar before Him daily and He begins to sooth our wounds and bring about our healing. The issue, however, is that the average Christian will never take a moment to stop and take inventory of their life up until this date, they will never look back and bring the knots of old before the Lord. Many are not even aware that they are knotted, they simply know something is not right but have no idea what that something is. The average pastor will know that He is called by the Lord and begin the process of preaching and teaching, never committing himself to a season of the unknotting of his soul, so that the dents and imprints of pain on his soul do not affect and contaminate the very platform that he so eagerly desires. I don't claim it to be all the time, but certainly sometimes, most times, looking back at our foundation will provide much answer to today's dysfunction.

Throughout the unknotting, the family, generational patterns, the source of knots and dysfunction will be discussed. We begin by looking at sources of dysfunction in an attempt to identify roots.

SECTION 1:
IDENTIFYING ROOTS

1

FAMILY UNDER SIEGE

I am certain we have all endured times when we have been too embarrassed to share our family's deepest secrets or family set up with our wider community. We have believed the lie that our family is a standout anomaly in the midst of what we consider normality. The movies, breakfast adverts, television and a perfectly staged hour spent at a friend's house has tricked us into believing that our set up is peculiar and odd. However, should we look long enough through our neighbour's perfectly pleated curtains, we come to find that this of course is incredibly far from the truth.

Our society is currently in dire chaos. Our police system, reform system, education system and our governments are out of God's perfect order. Although the smallest unit in society, the family is indeed the institution with the largest impact and ripple effect to the rest of society when it hits a road block, begins to fragment or completely fails in its duty. When a family breaks down the children of course feel its effects, but those that go on to interact with those children, marry those children, are birthed out of those children and communities where those children are raised are often those that suffer the greatest impact. The family's collapse is truly one of a domino effect on society as a whole.

When looking at gang culture in a city it is key to look at the type of children that end up in such a lifestyle of violence and defiance. Statistics worldwide have shown that it is often those that have grown up without fathers and (or) emotionally absent mothers, possibly with a track record of violence or criminal activity in the immediate or extended family. In order to attack a society, Satan has always had the tactic of getting to the family as a means to infect the wider community in his sinister bid to disrupt God's greater plan.

The Lord's plan for the family

If we all agree that our God is one that is full of wisdom, unlimited in power and the embodiment of creativity, then we can agree that whatever He creates is the best of its kind that could have existed. In all His wisdom, the

Lord chose not to have children born to a man and woman and then given over to different segments of society to be raised, or for a woman to give birth and join a part of society where all the mothers raised children together like some forms of the animal kingdom, no, our God

> *The family is a unit that works only when all members are committed to playing their role well.*

chose this peculiar and intimate structure called family. He chose one man with one woman to be fruitful and to multiply. He chose for a man and a woman to live together and raise their own children. He chose for the man to give instruction and for the woman to nurture and for the children to obey their parents in the Lord. Sounds pretty simple, right? Well it should be. Except the family is a unit that works only when *all* members are committed to playing their role well. When a father fails to give instruction, the family becomes lost and loses direction. When a mother fails to nurture, the family becomes cold and a house ultimately never becomes a home. When the children refuse to obey their parents, anarchy rises up and God's perfect order for the home is thrown out of the window. The enemy continues to be crafty in his attack of the family unit.

The very first attack on mankind was one of attempting to break the internal infrastructure by coming between the marriage union that God had put

The Unknotting

together. The Lord God gave instructions to Adam as to where he and his wife were to feed off; the serpent however, convinced Eve that something had been hidden from her, causing her to rebel against God's instructions to this first family on earth. The family unit hasn't been the same since this time.

The Bible is the best place to go to when looking at how the enemy has attacked the family overtime. Adam and Eve were a unified force, replenishing the earth, multiplying, having dominion and subduing the animals under their care until the fall of man occurred. Satan cornered the woman when she was apart from her husband and got into her ear. He was aware of the strength of unity and didn't dare approach the two when they stood together, he waited then baited until the weaker vessel was ready for prey. Though the serpent attacked Eve through his cunningness, the whole family unit suffered, her husband in turn fell victim to the attack and their perfect family picture in God's safe haven was no more. When one member in a household comes under attack, it often opens the door to chaos and dysfunction in the whole entire family structure. Adam and Eve lost eternal life, dominion and identity and following on from this attack in the garden, the family unit continued to come under siege.

Biblical account of families under attack.

Contrary to widespread belief, tension within the family is not a new phenomenon. We see stories of murder and strife even from the book of Genesis when Cain slew his own brother fuelled with envy over Abel's better and more acceptable sacrifice. We read about Joseph's own brothers selling him into slavery when consumed with jealousy and we learn of Jacob's tricking of his own brother for his birth right. Many more accounts of sexual perversion, rape and idolatry within the family unit is listed, such as the rape of Tamar by her own brother in the book of Samuel. The family has been and continues to be a target of the enemy. The question we can ask is, why?

How God uses the family for change

Nothing great has ever occurred in the earth without the Lord shining a light on a family in which to work through. When the father released Jesus into the earth He did so to a family. Mary was said to be promised to Joseph, he had not yet married her and had it in mind to put her out quietly. However, the Lord spoke with Joseph and Joseph took on the responsibility of raising Jesus as a part of *his* family. It was key for Jesus to be nurtured and trained by family, a mother to love and care for him, a father to mentor and teach him how to provide (eventually he became a carpenter just like his father joseph, we can assume he spent endless hours learning from his father the essential skills required). God chose family to do such a great work through. In the book of Exodus, He chose the older brother of Moses; Aaron and his descendants to work through and with, in order to establish his priesthood and act as mediators between God and man. God favours doing a work with the family structure. With the correct nurturing and appropriate guidance, mothers and fathers can raise incredible vessels fit for the Lord's use. Zachariah and Elizabeth did an incredible job raising John the Baptist, they raised Him so well that he fulfilled his call and realised his purpose. The Lord gave Samuel to a mother like Hannah, who He knew would do well to release him to be mentored by Eli that he may become a key prophetic voice to the nations. The family is used by God as a seedbed to plant the necessary seeds in a child that He would eventually use for His glory. Unfortunately, much of the parents in our world fail to realise this truth. They fail to understand that when the Lord releases a child into their care they hold the responsibility of ensuring that the necessary tools and keys that *this* particular child would need to fulfil destiny lie in their hands.

Though Satan has tried his hardest with the introduction of alternatives to the family unit such as the homosexual agenda, the transgender movement and the increase of the single parent household, advocates for the nuclear family still speak of its benefits. Much can be said for a child that has grown up with a present father, an emotionally whole and stable and care giving mother in an environment conducive for the Lord's presence to dwell.

Though considering all, how thankful we must be for a father who foreknew the enemy's plan and has gone ahead of us to make every crooked path straight. Though many of us may not have been raised in the perfect nuclear family, God can and God does make up the difference in the areas where we permit His doing so. Where parents have failed to guide, to nurture and to direct, He can step in as the parent we always required.

I have come to learn however, that sometimes, before we can ask the Lord to step in as something we never had, we must first humbly admit our brokenness and our need for mending.

A huge part of healing is knowing how we got hurt to begin with. For many of us, when the family unit that the Lord released us into failed us, it caused unspeakable levels of damage to our hearts, minds and outlooks on life. The effects of our childhood or family set up and generational background play a huge role in our adult decisions, choices and can ultimately determine the course of our lives. When we don't realise why the ship of our life seems to be veering off course, it's difficult to set it back on the correct path. However, when we shine a light on the root and not simply the fruit of dysfunction, we begin to see where we became broken and can take our brokenness to the ultimate healer and ask that He put us back together again.

2

CHILDREN OF FAILED MARRIAGES

"Where there is a problem child, there is a problem marriage"

- James L. Framo, journal of family and marital therapy, 1975

"Married couples are the bedrock of society"

- David Cameron, The Telegraph, 2015

"The Lord God said, "It is not good for the man to be alone. I will make a helper suitable for him." Now

the Lord God had formed out of the ground all the wild animals and all the birds in the sky. He brought them to the man to see what he would name them; and whatever the man called each living creature, that was its name. So the man gave names to all the livestock, the birds in the sky and all the wild animals.

But for Adam no suitable helper was found. So the Lord God caused the man to fall into a deep sleep; and while he was sleeping, he took one of the man's ribs and then closed up the place with flesh. Then the Lord God made a woman from the rib he had taken out of the man, and he brought her to the man.

The man said, "This is now bone of my bones and flesh of my flesh; she shall be called 'woman,' for she was taken out of man." That is why a man leaves his father and mother and is united to his wife, and they become one flesh. Adam and his wife were both naked, and they felt no shame."

- Genesis 2: 18-25, NIV

What a beautiful account of the joining together of the very first marital union on earth. For Adam, no suitable mate was found but the one that was bone of his bone and flesh of his flesh. None was found outside of him, so the Lord God brought the perfect one from within him, no companion could fill his longing but that which perfectly resembled him. The joining of one man to one woman, God's very own design, His very own institution, His perfect order and design for mankind, marriage; the absolute prototype for success, the "bedrock of society" as rightly noted by former UK Prime Minister, David Cameron. When perfectly executed it is indeed the recipe for success, when mishandled however, broken marriages do more than damage the two individuals that consented to the union, it sends a ripple effect of pain and trauma to the generations that were birthed out of the union.

> *Broken marriages do more than damage the two individuals that consented to the union.*

If you are the product of a broken marriage, much of the dysfunction that you have noted in your life could very well be a direct result of a broken covenant between the man and the woman that played a vital role in your existence.

Looking at where we come from is a key part to obtaining freedom. Though Jesus saves our spirit, we must bring our soul before Him that we may be washed a new. Much of that washing is identifying how we got dirty in the first place. In order to obtain true freedom, we must travel down the road of our existence and allow the Lord to minister healing to the damaged little boy or girl within.

Much of the Bible's accounts of Jesus performing miracles are those of physical ailment or demonic manifestations. However, one of my favourite accounts in the bible is found in John 4 where we see Jesus have an account with an unknown woman at a well in Samaria. The woman; in need of water as she stood by the well failed to realise the reason for her lifelong thirst, Jesus not only freed her, He showed her the root of her dysfunction, He explained to her about her deep desire for love and acceptance, a longing she attempted to fill with male relationships, resulting in multiple failed marriages. Do you know that Jesus could have just told this woman who He was, performed a miracle and claimed another follower there and then? But He desired so much more than that, He desired more than followers and believers, He desired and still desires free people. He desired to free this woman's soul from patterns of dysfunction, He desired to fill her with truth by first shining a light on the lies that she had believed. He led her down memory lane by forcing her to recollect memories of failed marriages, to confront her current state and to admit her dysfunction before true healing could even begin. The Lord demands the same of you and I. Looking at the marriage of the two people that gave you a start to life is a great place to start.

God's original plan for marriage between a man and a woman was to be a reflection of Christ and His love for His bride. The family was to be a self-contained source of learning.

For many, their family home and parents' marriage is where they learn love and affection, it's their very first lesson in team work. A marriage of two individuals was designed to be the place where their offspring learn and become accustomed to the fundamentals of this world. The fundamental and key ingredients to survival should and must come from viewing our parents' marriage as the very first institution we behold. Our initial life lessons often come from our parents.

However, for many of us, our parents' marriage and family home taught us fear, it taught us chaos, manipulation and disrespect. For many, our parents' marriage taught us what a lack of honour was, what a man stepping out on his wife meant, what it looked like to watch "love" strike its spouse with a hand or an object, to infect its spouse with a deadly sexual disease, to cause weeping well into the night or to leave financially tangled and enslaved to sleeping pills or high blood pressure. I heard a story from a young lady whose father ripped the very hair off her mother's scalp. This should not be so. A marriage of the two people that brought us to life was created to be our safe haven, our safe place, our very first rescue hub where we find peace and belonging.

To witness the above, on any level, even verbal disrespect, is to have our soul subject to dysfunction from an age so young that we are unable to barricade ourselves from its effects. Witnessing the above as a child alters and falsifies our perception of love. Whether we choose to allow it or not, the effects of coming from such dysfunction will show up in our personalities, in our thought process, in the way that we view the world, in the way that we view the Lord and even our view of fatherhood, motherhood and marriage.

I remember being 12 years old and running up the communal stairs of our then flat. On my way home from school and dressed in full uniform attire, I ran so hard up the stairs that I landed on my face but got up as though nothing had happened, I was determined to save my mother from the sounds of violence. I ran into the flat, ready to shout, "stop fighting!" only to find that the noise of violence that I had heard was only within my own head. There *was* no fight. In fact, my mother was home alone. You see I had become so accustomed to being a child begging her parents to stop the fight *(an unfortunate norm for many children)* that I had actually began to hear the sounds of shouting and violence even in the midst of silence. Fear had so creeped into my life that it had become a part of me. Over the years in my life, I found that I became controlling, a trait that no doubt came from always trying to control my parent's behaviour or the atmosphere of my home in a bid to avoid raised voices.

I recall being 9 years old and hearing a family member call my mother to inform her of a woman who had been killed by her partner in a fight between the two in their home. I recall my mum's passing sound of shock, I heard it in her voice that she feared this becoming her fate if one day their "arguments" got out of hand. I remember being 9 years old and internalising that fear. Often for years following that moment, I realise now that I developed the habit of walking past my mother's room and stopping outside her door for a few seconds to ensure that I saw the covers rise and fall; proof that she was still alive and breathing, a responsibility that I took upon myself. I noticed over the years that I would also do this with other family members, ensuring they were still breathing, as though their breath was at my control, as though if I failed to do so then something sinister could have happened to them. Fear and false responsibility had truly gripped my heart.

The enemy of my soul, the devil himself, used

this spell in my life as an open door to grip me with the spirit of fear, to invite in false thoughts and elaborated thoughts of violence and death, a spirit of control and a desperate desire to always remain "safe". Open doors that He then used as gateways of attack to inflict in adulthood a range of fear based moments. Saved yes, in ministry yes, laying hands on others yes, but until I dealt with the wounds in my soul by allowing the Lord to unknot the tangled mess of the past, freedom was very far from me.

I wonder what open doors were created in your childhood as a result of your parents' marriage that are now being used as gateways of attack in your life as an adult? Could the anxiety be a result of a fearful childhood? Could the depression be internalised shame or a lack of identity?

Childhood scars and triggers

Triggers are something that cause a reaction or emotion that lay dormant within us to come to the surface. Often times, the pains and scars of our childhood lay within us but we fail to acknowledge how deep the scar runs until an event occurs that triggers the pain of our past. For some of us, it's not until we are preparing for our own marriage that we find how fearful we are of commitment because the example we had or didn't have left an imprint of pain and such hurt on our soul.

For me, I found that I had a fear that it may be impossible for a man to love me and only me. What I had experienced in my family home taught me that one woman was never enough for a man, in fact two or three women were not enough either.

Traits of children of failed marriages

Repeating the cycle

For many children of failed marriages, they often vow not to repeat the cycle of the loveless home that they have come from yet find themselves continuing on the cycle. It is easy for such a continual pattern when the root of the dysfunction is not identified yet bitterness is harboured or a vow not to repeat the same cycle is made, but Christ is not invited in to break the chains of old. No amount of tongue speaking or worship atmosphere can take the place of the unknotting. Cycles will be repeated when children of failed marriages fail to stop and examine the patterns that led to the failed marriages in their generational line. For example, I had noted in my generational line, women would set up home with men who failed to be husbands worthy of being called fathers. The men would father children with them and then leave them as single mothers. I had the potential of running the same trait had I not noticed the pattern and began to pray into generational patterns and began to ask the Lord to break the cycle in me by helping me to make God ordained decisions when it comes to marriage and settling down.

Fear of failure

Children of failed marriages often carry the fear of failure. Watching what should be one of our greatest successes to witness as a child; the marriage of our parents fail, can lead a child to experience an innate fear of failure. Very often we find that witnessing such a failure can make us fearful of replicating the same thing in our own marriages or lives. When children are left in a broken home and grow up, for example with a single mother, they may watch their mother struggle financially and vow to themselves to create a better life for their mother and their siblings. A responsibility that was never ordained by the Lord to fall upon the child, but upon the father of the home. A child is then forced to take upon themselves a task that is simply not ordained for them and walk in shoes several sizes too big for them. A fear of failure grips such a child and an unhealthy level of ambition becomes their companion. Dysfunctional modes of thoughts and patterns have found their place with fear being the driving force. Whilst most children of successful marriages attend university with little pressure but achieving a great grade, children of failed marriages bare the pressure of ensuring a great career or early age success in order to free their family from a life of struggle. When they fail to achieve early age success or reach the pinnacle of financial freedom at the desired age, they may feel a sense of failure. This was never God's order or design. This, is the work of the enemy of our soul, who has managed to gain entry into a child's outlook on life through the breakdown of the child's parent's marriage.

> *"A good man leaves an inheritance to his children's children, ..."*
> *(Proverbs 13:22, AMP)*

The Lord's perfect order is not that a child bare the financial responsibility of their parent or parents throughout a marital breakdown, but that a good man leave an inheritance for not only his child but his children's children. Dysfunction has caused us to have a skewed perception of what honour looks like in our generation.

False responsibility

Children of failed marriages can often suffer from a strong sense of false responsibility. Their lives, at times, are not truly being lived with them and the Lord in mind. Their way of living may not particularly be their first desire, but they do what they need to do to make their parent or household proud, or to move them out of poverty or emotional lack. This happens even to those serving Christ. Their service can often be tainted or laced with the taste of success being a benefit to not only the Kingdom of God, but their family also. Such an inroad could be used by the enemy to corrupt such a sacred call. I remember a time when a friend of mine that had the opportunity to live in the States playing American football, an incredible happening for an 18-year-old, but one he didn't take, however, because his mother and his sister would have been left alone. A beautiful and thoughtful gesture of course, but I can't help but wonder if he would have taken this opportunity had he come from a home where his mother and father were happily married.

Fear of true love

Having seen what false love looks like, children of failed marriages often fear *true* love. They may fear it as they've never witnessed it or experienced it. I am assured of this to be the reason why those coming from single parent families, or homes where a parent's marriage was less than stable, find it hard to allow the Lord in as a loving Father. For those that have not embraced the love of an earthly father it is beyond their comprehension to grasp the unconditional love of an unseen father. The word 'father' may denote fear or violence or absentee in their own mind's record of what they have known a father to be. Fear of true love becomes a deep knot when looking at dysfunction.

Fear of exposure or transparency

For children of failed marriages that came from a home full of violence or secrets, transparency becomes a huge task. For individuals like this, the root to their lack of openness or transparency may be traced back to times of secret keeping in a household, times of covering up at school and pretending all was well though they endured mayhem just the night before.

Mental health

Children who grow up in a broken home are often said to be more at risk of suffering from mental illness categorised symptoms or diagnosis later in life. Using fear, emotional baggage or a lack of love and affection as an inroad to a child's mind, Satan will often stand prey over such individuals awaiting the perfect moment to reel in his bait.

Dysfunction categorised by the failure of a parent's marriage is a clear indication of a shaky foundation and knots being embedded in the early life of a child.

Building a picture and gaining understanding as you read, we'll go on to talk about the effects of fatherlessness in the life of a child. How does a lack of fatherhood affect you and I as full grown Christian adults in today's world?

3

PATERNAL TIES

"Children's children are the crown of old men; and the glory of children are their Fathers"

- Proverbs 17:6

If the glory (high renown and honour) of children are their fathers, then the question beckons, what honour is had by those that grew up without their fathers?

Think back to the school playground, when kids played the boastful game of "my dad's better than your dad", no one ever did say "my mum's stronger than your mum", it was the strength of their father that a child would boast in. The moments when their father could lift them up in the air and spin them around with what looked like loose caution, the moments

> *What honour is had by those that grew up without their fathers?*

of wrestling with dad and being tossed in the air on a summer's day in the park were the moments in a child's life that led one to boast of the powerful strength of a Father. In the Greek language, the word glory translates to 'doxa' meaning "weight" or "heaviness". Another way of describing the substance of a thing, how weighty (full of substance) a thing is. For a child therefore, their Father was, and for many continues to be, their crowning glory (their substance) as Proverbs 17:6 rightfully describes. For those that were not afforded the privilege to grow with their father; they're those that walked around crownless as a child, a crownless state that often follows one into adulthood.

Identity

To walk around without a crown is to walk around as a pauper, whilst the crowned glide in their rightful identity as kings and queens. It is to imagine a school playground full of young royals and the few walking around crownless are those unaware of their high-class state. They are those that have no daddy to go home to or have never known their father. By reason of Christ as our king, you and I are indeed royalty, but of course we do not know this as a young girl or boy, even yet as men and women; not until we begin to walk in close communion with the Lord and learn of our true identity. So where does our identity initially come from?

The Hebrew word for 'father' is the word 'Abba' which translates to mean source. That is to say, for every child born into the earth their father is their source. The male man is initially the source for life as the sperm ignites the female egg upon fertilisation and the female simply acts as a carrier (this being the reason why we can have surrogacy and see a woman carry another couple's baby in her own womb yet she may not be the biological mother; but never has it been seen that a man borrow another man's sperm and still remain the biological father). The woman was always designed to act as the carrier and the male man functions as the kick starter of life, the source from which life begins. This role of being the source (the well from which all information is drawn) was always reserved for and can only be played by the male. Our fathers (our source) are therefore the fountain from which we draw our identity.

> *To remove a father from the home is to remove a child's identity.*

When we take on our Father's surname at birth, we bare the mark of who they are, we declare that this is the lineage from which we came, it's our identity, it's who we are. When looking at Proverbs 17:6, it therefore becomes glaringly obvious that to remove a father from the home is to remove a child's identity, it is to leave a child exposed without a covering.

For many adult Christians, paternal ties in the form of a lack of fatherhood continues to be our greatest battle. In this chapter, we will look closely at the effects and analysis of a home without a father.

Fatherless homes

When we refer to some adult men or women and state that they have "daddy issues", what we actually mean to say is they have an issue of a lack of identity. Growing up in a fatherless home or with a physically present yet absent in heart and mind father has led them to grow up without a crown, essentially leaving them not knowing their identity as royalty, a lack of information which could cause one to live below their appointed standard.

I remember the Lord once said to me, *"For every girl growing up without a father is attacked with a spirit of prostitution, a spirit that causes one to sell themselves below their value".* What a travesty that our young women, when not affirmed and crowned rightly by their fathers, go on to give themselves away for prices less than their value.

The role of a father

For many the role of a father is viewed simply as being a provider (hence why we have some very hard-working fathers that are never at home, but will always ensure the bills and private tuition fees are paid). Worse still, we have the fathers that were simply sperm givers and nothing more, or those that care to see about their children only once every few years.

The role of a father extends much further than sperm giver, provider or even the playground air toss and wrestling bouts. The number one role of a father is that of affirmation. A father is to affirm their child and provide them with a solid identity. By the very physical presence of a father being in the same home as their child, without even uttering a word of prayer, their stance alone acts as a shield over the child. No mother, no matter how great, can fulfil this role, only a male man has the authority to cover his home in the way predestined for a man to do so by the Lord. A male model in a child's life taking up the totality of a fatherhood role can at times also suffice. We witness this in the book of Esther with her cousin Mordecai who stepped in as her male father figure and groomed and prepared her for what would be her life's purpose. Men willing to step into a young child's life as father are a true blessing, as to leave this father role totally unmet is where we find wide doors of chaos.

> *"This is my beloved son, in whom I am well pleased?" (Matthew 3:17)*

We witness the greatest father-son relationship in Christ Jesus and God the Father. Before Christ had performed any miracles, before He had been revealed to many as the promised messiah, His Father let out a raw from Heaven and let all creation know, *"This is My beloved Son"*. When a son is aware of his father's pride and joy in him, not for anything he has done, but simply by reason of his existence, it does something incredible to the self-esteem of the child. In essence, if my daddy said it, then it must be true.

Study from psychologists Paquette and Bigras, 2010, shows that paternal involvement is associated with increased self confidence in a child. The psychologist.bps.org.uk also highlights the following relating to absent fathers:

> *"Because fathers more than mothers often encourage children to push boundaries (Brussoni & Olsen, 2011), father involvement is also associated with less fear of failure (Teevan et al., 1986) and higher self-esteem (Harper*

& Ryder, 1986) relative to children who grow up without their biological father. Male parental investment of time and money is also linked with a number of desirable social outcomes, including greater academic achievement in childhood, higher socio-economic status (SES) in adulthood, and increased upward social mobility (Amato, 1998; DeBell, 2008; Geary, 2005; Kaplan et al., 1998; Mulkey et al., 1992).

Not surprisingly, whereas the presence of one's father is found to have a positive influence on developmental outcomes, father absence is reliably associated with a variety of dubious psychological dispositions and social outcomes. For instance, research has demonstrated that children from father-absent homes are less able to delay gratification than children from two-parent homes (Mischel et al., 1989). They also demonstrate more interpersonal problems, poorer psychological adjustment, and more depression and anxiety than boys and girls from intact families (Jane Costello et al., 2006). As young adults, they consume more alcohol (Kenny & Schreiner, 2009), are more likely to be incarcerated (Anderson et al., 2002) and demonstrate more hostile behaviours relative to youth growing up with their biological father. Finally, many of these risks appear to be heightened for children and adolescents who – in addition to father absence – lack a positive relationship with their mother (Mason et al., 1994)"[2]

Why is God Father?

Today I came across a short clip of a Muslim woman who stated that the only difference between Islam and Christianity is who we view Jesus to be. She claimed Jesus could not be the Son of God as God is not a Father but a Holy God. Whilst there are of course much more differences in our faith than this alone, we can rest on this point for a moment.

Firstly, without Jesus coming to earth there would be no remission of sin, there would be no

---

[2] https://thepsychologist.bps.org.uk/volume-29/june/absent-fathers-and-sexual-strategies

forgiveness, but more importantly we would not know God as the greatest attribute that He desires to be known by; Father. Christ came to reveal a Holy and feared God as a loving Father. Jesus could have referred to God the Father as Master, Ruler, Judge or the many other most powerful attributes that He carries. But you see, the world already knew Him as all of these in the Old Testament, they had seen Him part the red sea, provide manner in the wilderness, rain down as fire from above, yet sin was still prevalent and righteousness was scarce. However, when Christ came to reveal God as Father, love entered into the hearts of men and hardened hearts were softened by the Spirit which allows us to cry out, not righteous judge, but Abba Father (see Romans 8:15). When God was revealed as Father (in the image of His Son) seas no longer parted, fire didn't rain down from above. but blind eyes began to open, the deaf heard, the dead were raised and the lost found their way home. The emotionally broken, like the woman in John 4 by the well in Samaria, found healing for their wounded hearts, outcast lepers were healed back into civilisation and the rich, wise men and paupers all found themselves on the same playing field in desperate need of the fatherhood of God. I am assured that being fathered correctly makes the world of difference in the heart and life of the average child.

    The truth is, many religions in the world have no problem with Christianity, in fact they tolerate and welcome it. Contention and division only arises when it comes to the very attribute of God that can change our lives; He is our Father! He lives through His only begotten Son who is the head of the body (See Colossians 1:18). It is no surprise to me that the world struggles to see God as Father. To know God as judge, holy or majesty requires no intimacy, oh but to know Him as Father, your heart must be engaged. But it's hard for human beings to know God as the very attribute that we are being cultured to believe we *can* live without. One of the great attacks on mankind at the moment is that of Fatherhood. Difficulty arises for human beings who have not been fathered well to understand a loving God as the very attribute they know as "deadbeat", "absentee", "sperm donor", "baby daddy"; all of the connotations that our society currently has with the word father. If God had come to reveal Himself as mother, I have no doubt our world would have done a better job at receiving Him, it's no surprise that Hollywood celebrates "Mother Nature "or "Mother Earth" but rejects Father God. We as a people have been cultured (whether by society or our very own family situation of a missing father) to hate fatherhood. Yet, fatherhood is the only thing that will save us. It is the key to our identity. It is the revelation of our existence.

> *Much of our dysfunction as adults comes from the lack of fatherhood.*

Much of our dysfunction as adults comes from the lack of fatherhood. Many men struggle with pornography because of a lack of fatherhood. Strip clubs are filled with our young women exposing their bodies for currency due to a lack of fatherhood. Young boys and girls are in gangs because of a lack of fatherhood. Prisons are full in cities across the world because of fatherhood.

When Adam and Eve sinned against God in Genesis 3, they ultimately declared their independence; Christ came to restore the fatherhood of God, that you and I may walk with our heads held high knowing that our crown is our Father, our identity is in our fatherhood.

Christ the high esteemed Son

When I read through the gospels I see a Jesus high in esteem, high in confidence, not lacking in His identity, I see a Son who knew exactly who He was, His identity as a beloved Son of His Father was never in question. He didn't suffer from knots of dysfunction through paternal ties. How did Christ achieve this and how can you and I achieve this?

His Father told Him

"This is my beloved son, in whom I am well pleased?" (Matthew 3:17)

We have all seen the short clips of talk shows such as Oprah or Dr Phil in which a father and son duo come out to speak on their estranged relationship. Often times, the adult son (who may now have children of his own) breaks down in tears and tells his father, "I just needed to hear you say well done son". No matter our age or our position in life, it is essential to our esteem and identity that we hear our fathers affirm us.

Unlike earthly fathers, God the Father didn't leave it up to chance, He affirmed His Son. He told His Son that He was pleased with Him, He reminded Him that He was His offspring, we can assume both privately and of course publicly. He gave Him positive affirmation. Why? Because just a chapter later in Matthew 4 the very identity of Jesus would be tested when Satan would come to Him and taunt, "if you are the Son of God?" (See Matthew 4:1-11).

The world will also test your identity. Circumstances will come and have already come along to test and see if you know who you are. If you had not been affirmed by a loving father you would have failed that test. Jesus passed the test in Matthew 4 because His Father had pre-affirmed Him in Matthew 3. For you and I, tests of our identity don't often come in satanic encounters, they come in day to day life.

"For every woman who lives without a father falls prey to the spirit of

prostitution, a spirit which causes one to sell oneself below their value"

As mentioned earlier, the above is what the Lord spoke to my heart a few months ago. If you are a female child growing up without a father, the likelihood of you having sexual experiences with men in your teen years or early twenties (men most likely who you knew wouldn't commit to you and simply desired your body) is very high. The moment the opportunity to say yes or no to the advances of what I call stray men presented itself, could be viewed as one of life's tests to see if you knew your identity. Failure of such a test is often due to a lack of fatherhood.

The psychology PIT theory (Paternal Investment Theory) was looked into by psychologists Sarah E. Hill, Randy P. Proffitt Laya and Danielle J. Priore in their publication "Absent Father's and sexual strategies"[3]. They found that, "women expressed greater acceptance of – and greater willingness to engage in – casual sexual relationships after describing their father's absence".[4] The study found that paternal investment (how present ones father is and how far he invests in the child's life) is linked to the sexual attitude of the female child.

---

[3] https://docs.wixstatic.com/ugd/5ff4b9_7d7c3b0a24f34033914021962bb24b21.pdf
[4] https://docs.wixstatic.com/ugd/5ff4b9_7d7c3b0a24f34033914021962bb24b21.pdf

Watch and repeat

"Very truly I tell you, the Son can do nothing by himself, he can only do what he sees his father doing, because whatever the father does the son also does" (John 5:19, NIV)

For the male child growing up without a father this statement speaks volumes. Here Jesus indicates that fatherhood is studied. What a Son sees his father do, he is bound to repeat. We have all heard the story of the son who grew up watching his father beat his mother and vowed that he would never hit his own wife, yet bruises and a home filled with violence or momentary outburst of anger torments his own life. Though the son has every desire not to be like his father, he repeats that which he has seen. For men that had emotionally absent fathers, they too can find it hard to show love and affection to their own children, or for the son with the promiscuous father, commitment to one woman could be a battle. All examples are fulfilling the words of Christ above, what a son sees his father do, he also is likely to repeat.

When the head leaves – Satan attacks

With the father being the spiritual head of a home, many of us believe that once a father leaves the home the woman automatically steps up as the head, this is not so. Should a man willingly leave his family home (not taken away by death and the family graced for such a portion), and that position isn't filled by another, he leaves his seat unfilled and increases the likelihood of satanic activity against his family. Statistics show that children from broken homes are more likely to watch pornography from an early age, engage in criminal or gang related activity, have teen pregnancies and in more sinister minority cases engage in incest. This is not a coincidence. When a man willingly walks away from his family he increases their risk of the above.

Identifying paternal ties

The discussions above may have led you to think of dysfunction that may be showing up in your present adult life through paternal ties, possibly from an absent father, an emotionally absent father or a father you never knew. You may possibly struggle with a lack of affirmation, a lack of self-confidence or self-belief and shy away from taking risks in life (all traits of a lack of fatherhood); your dysfunction may even run deeper in the form of failed marriages, a violent home, a promiscuous life style or mental and emotional instability due to your lack of fatherhood.

Dysfunction can show up as fruits in our lives but many of us never stop to find the root. For you, paternal ties in the form of a lack of fatherhood may be the seed that has caused such dysfunctional fruit to appear in your adulthood. It may have been or continues to be hard for you to accept God the Father due to the bad example of fatherhood you have experienced in your own life. A comforting thought is of course the truth that by the means of adoption we now have a Heavenly Father to call our very own (see Romans 8:15), but the pains of our earthly father and their lack of involvement in our lives could still be showing up as imprints on our soul. As you continue reading, healing will come and by reason of your acknowledgement, I pray the unknotting will begin to take place.

> *Dysfunction can show up as fruits in our lives but many of us never stop to find the root.*

4

MATERNAL TIES

Whilst dysfunction can take place through our paternal line, just as great a damage may occur through our maternal line via our mothers. Maternal ties refer to forms of dysfunction (in thinking patterns or day to day life) of which we can trace their roots back to our relationship or lack thereof with our mothers.

Maternal ties causing dysfunction can take place through some of the scenarios discussed below.

Single mothers as fathers

In the previous chapter we discussed absent fathers.

With the unfortunately high number of single parent families in our society, more women are making the dysfunctional move of stepping in as both mother and father to their children. I recall hearing many single mothers in my own family always making the point to remind the children that they were both "mummy and daddy". A statement of sentiment and a lovely gesture, but a tool of the enemy to cause chaos in the future of a child.

The roles of both mother and father are incredibly different and are set as such to only be fulfilled by the appropriate God ordained gender. The mother to nurture; the father to affirm. The mother to teach a girl how to be a woman; the father to exemplify being a man to his son.

With single mothers set out and intent on having their child not miss out on having a father, they attempt to step into the role of both functions. In my own home, I saw the impossibility of such an attempt when my older brother reached 6"3 and towered over my mother, her efforts to be both "mummy and daddy" failing woefully. As great as she was in being mother, the truth is mothers make diabolical fathers. Why? Because women were never created to *father* their children, it's not in their make up

{ *Women were never created to father their children.* }

to do so. It's as though one were to ask a pencil to function as a chair, it's impossible, it would be painful and incredibly dysfunctional.

Attitudes in the child

Growing up in a home such as this can create attitudes of dysfunction in the child which tend to show up in our lives as adults.

I don't need a father

For the most part, many children who grow up in this type of environment live their childhood and adult lives believing, "*I don't need a father*". This was my attitude for a long time. I truly believed and would actually sit on stages and comment "*I had such a great mother I didn't notice that I didn't have a father, I was fine.*" But this couldn't be further from the truth. Though I did indeed have a great mother, and though I possibly didn't notice my father's absence, I was far from fine. Affirmation was lacking, daddy daughter days were lacking, my crown (see chapter 2) was lacking, my viewpoint of fatherhood and men was skewed, my actions and decisions, my crippling low self-esteem and self-consciousness were all signs of an internal dysfunction. It is no surprise then that statistics show that girls who tend to grow up like this end up marrying or having relationships with men like the very fathers they claim they didn't need. In the souls bid to find the fulfilment of the father that it never had, it is likely that it seeks out a man just like daddy to heal wounds that were never seen.

Women can successfully raise a child alone

Another dysfunctional lie that children who have grown up in such an environment can end up believing is the above. For many females in particular, who grow up in a single parent home, they too go on to have children with men and raise their own children alone. An underlying thought that goes something like this leads their relationships, *"if he leaves I can do this alone, my mum did it alone"*. Thoughts that end up shaping their decisions in partner choices and leaves them not fighting as hard as they could have done in their marriage or relationship to ensure that their children be raised by both parents (should the circumstances have permitted). Children in this instance become a form of reward or prized possession and are of a higher importance than one's marriage, continuing on a legacy of dysfunction. Now, can a single mother successfully raise a child alone? She sure can raise a child which goes on to achieve success; however, she cannot possibly go on to raise a child (with no father or father figure) which grows to be a whole and well-balanced individual with zero traces of dysfunction (no matter how little or great) at some point or points in their life.

Evidence of a lack of fatherhood will always show up at some time or season or worse still, it will plague the life of the child. If mothers were able to raise a child alone then the Lord would not have deemed His functioning normal to be that of family. I encourage single mothers to make a conscious effort to have their children around trusted male role models, grandfathers, mentors or uncles able to step into the role of a father as much as possible. I don't encourage what some attempt to do, which is to enter into a relationship with a man unfit for the title husband, in their bid to forcefully find a fatherhood replacement for their child. If you are a single mother, look out for traits of dysfunction in your child, be it low self-esteem, rejection, a craving for attention, make them prayer points in covering your child and I encourage conversation with your child or the fatherhood male role models in their life.

> *If mothers were able to raise a child alone then the Lord would not have deemed His functioning normal to be that of family.*

Married to my children

For some, maternal ties cause dysfunction in their lives when single mothers take it upon their children (especially their male sons) to act as their replacement husband. This comes in the form of caring for and having emotional relations with sons in the same form that a woman would have with her husband. Ross Rosenberg, author of *The Human Magnet Syndrome: Why we love people who hurt us*, describes enmeshed parent-child relationships. This is where parents and their children rely on one another to ultimately fulfil their emotional needs. Rosenberg describes how this form of soothing sacrifices psychological health. Clinical psychologist Dr Kenneth M. Adams, Ph.D. has written a book titled, *Silently Seduced: When parents make their children partners.* Dr Adams deals greatly with offering tools for identifying and healing from covert incestuous relationships. He explains in the book how feeling close with a parent is of course not a source of comfort especially when the child is cheated out of their own childhood. This can of course take place when healthy boundaries of a parent child relationship are not enforced when a mother is left alone with none but her children to meet her emotional needs.

Effects on the son

The effect of this on the male son doesn't show up as dysfunctional often times until he either enters into a serious relationship or marries his own wife. I once sat through a groom's speech on his wedding day and heard him talk of his single mother, he proceeded to say, *"she's my queen, no one can take the place of my queen*", whilst his new wife sat beside him, I can only imagine she was digesting the fact she may have to settle for the place of "princess" seeing as his mother's place as queen remains undefeated.

Such thought patterns often arise in the son of a single mother who may have made it known that she played both mother and father role, or even in one who made no such declarations but failed to establish healthy parent-child boundaries. The son may feel a sense of betrayal towards the mother whom he acted as a replacement husband for, he can't possibly have a new queen, *who would now be king to his mother*? This ultimately causes a new pattern of dysfunction in his own home as the wife ultimately knows that she doesn't come first, her position *is* high, but will never be *as* high as the mother who *suffered* to raise him alone. They will eventually have children who will also learn the dysfunctional pattern that one's mother comes before one's wife.

"I can't leave, but I want to cleave."

"It is for this reason that a man must leave his mother and father and cleave to his wife"

- *Genesis 2:24*

For those raised in single parent households they tend to have a higher form of loyalty (not to be mistaken with bond) with their family members. They have been raised with the *"we only have one another"* mentality which causes a close unit but the closeness can at times be created out of dysfunction and not pure love. It isn't the beautiful moments of times spent at the park as a family or family dinners and holidays that have caused a closeness, for most single parent households it's the moments of possibly not much food to eat, bills not being paid or breakdown in family communication that has pushed them towards closeness. We can call it a false sense of loyalty. For this reason, children of single parent households will tend to find it harder than their peers from two parent households to perform the duties of Genesis 2:24 which is to firstly leave their family home (both physically and more so emotionally) before cleaving to their new spouse. For many, their loyalty to their single parent family home means that they may leave physically but struggle to leave in their heart, causing a diabolical dysfunction in their new home, as one cannot possibly cleave to the new until he has firstly completely left the old.

Are you in a marriage where your spouse is struggling to completely let go of his family? Maybe you have been married for years and the tie between he and his mother (or she and her mother) causes problems in your marriage, you may want to consider some of the above points as topics of conversation...

Absentee mothers

Whilst mothers at home acting as fathers can be dysfunctional, mothers who walk away from their children and leave them without maternal care can cause severe pain to the heart of their children.

For mothers taken away by death and unable to raise their children, I believe the Lord releases grace for these families, though it is sure that, dependent on the individual scenario, the children may still feel the sting in their adult life. For mothers however, who willingly walk away from their children, such a rejection knows no rival.

Can a woman forget her sucking child, that she should not have compassion on the son of her womb? yea, they may forget, yet will I not forget thee. (Isaiah 49:15)

If the Lord likens His love for us to a mother nursing her child, a bond unbreakable, can you imagine the pain and rejection that a child must feel when their own mother willingly walks away from them? I am guessing for some of you it takes no imagination as this is your reality. A reality that of course mirrors dysfunction. It is in essence somewhat unnatural to have a mother unwilling to care for her own child or put the needs of her child first. It is for this reason we would do well to look into the past of that mother, what pain or dysfunctional patterns have taken place in such a mother's life to cause her to inflict such a level of rejection on her own child?

If maternal ties and a lack of proper mothering or nurturing have caused you to feel rejected or worse still, unwanted, we will spend some time further on into the reading looking at rejection and tools to freedom.

SECTION 2: EFFECTS OF DYSFUNCTION

5

KNOTS, MARRIAGES & FAMILIES

One way in which dysfunction from our childhood can show up in our lives as adults is when bruised and damaged children grow to set up their own marital homes. For the majority of those who have identified with dysfunction stemming from previous chapters of this book such as being the child of a failed marriage, fatherlessness or maternal ties, without the process of the unknotting in one's single years, this dysfunction is promised to surface in one's marriage.

I once sat through marriage counselling with a young couple. I entered into their pristine home and was greeted by a wife that was the woman of most men's dreams; mesmerizingly beautiful, young, keeper of the home and a great mother to the couple's four children. The husband; young, somewhat handsome, fortunate to have such a woman and blessed to be at the position that he had found himself in life. I had been called in to counsel the couple by the wife after much persuasion to her husband following a season of infidelity and an overall bad spell in their six-year old marriage. The wife, I believe, had invited me in to counsel their marriage with an expectation for me to lay into her husband and give some biblical home truths as to why his behaviour in their marriage had been less than acceptable and then persuade him to treat and love his wife better. The counselling session did not go that way at all.

As I entered into their home, I had no idea what the Lord would have me speak on or how, I simply uttered a prayer that the Lord lead me as I walked through the doors. The session began with light joking as I believe the couple were indeed nervous, the man more so than the woman although he had little need to be. Shockingly, as I began the session, the Lord began to deal with the wife and her short comings. She was

> *The Lord will often always point the mirror to our own self in His bid to save us from ourselves.*

dumbfounded. The husband flabbergasted. I was not.

One thing I have come to learn in the process of the unknotting is that the Lord will often always point the mirror to our own self in His bid to save us from ourselves. It is imperative, especially in the area of marriage, that we allow Him to do this. If we agree that most of us in the world are living with foundational and occasional knots and knots in our soul, then it must be true that these knots do affect our marriages and relationships today.

Knots and entering into marriage

When dealing with the woman in the example above, one thing that the Lord really began to deal with was her reason for wanting to get married in the first place. You see to deal with knots we must always turn back in time and deal with our hearts intentions and state of mind at the time of the event in question. For many women dealing with foundational knots (dysfunction that takes place in one's infant years), they often view marriage as the hospital where all their wounds become healed; what they are in fact doing is creating a dumpsite where all their inner pains shall be revealed and poured unto the other party.

For the woman in my example above, the key in this session was to return to her childhood and her upbringing. She had been unwanted by her natural parents and grew up in dysfunction. She eventually grew to be found by a man who wanted her and settled down to marry. A Christian she was, but a wounded woman who had yet to deal with her past she was also. I remember a time in a prayer session with believers and hearing them refer to this young wife as "the perfect Proverbs 31 woman". On the surface, she was the home maker, the perfect wife who kept up her physical appearance and looked after her home with ease and with class. To others she was the standard to be looked up to. For me, I saw a woman who had taught herself how to maintain perfection out of a deep fear of losing the family she now had; the family that she as a child had always wanted and craved but never received. Her foundational knots were now appearing in her marriage, undealt with and unloosed knots were damaging the very thing that she was fighting so hard to keep. Knots in the soul will cause you to do the right things for all the wrong reasons.

> *Knots in the soul will cause you to do the right things for all the wrong reasons.*

What does this have to do with her husband's affair and overall bad behaviour I hear you say? Everything! You see a marriage of two knotted individuals creates a diabolical environment fit for dysfunction to dwell and make its home. Let's go unto the husband before looking at how both knots affect one another.

Upon speaking to the husband as the Lord led me, I pointed out a time (through prophetic utterance) of a dysfunctional moment in his childhood. What exactly happened to him I have no idea as the Lord didn't tell me that part, but whatever it was, the word given was enough to reduce him to tears. The wife intervened to ask her husband if this was the event in his life that they had spoken about previously. The husband's response was, *"no, I haven't told anyone about this, not even myself"*. You see dysfunctional knots can be so deep and dark that we completely bury them to the back of our minds and can truly begin to believe that they never occurred, though the very fruits of the event affect us day in and day out in our most intimate of relationships. The husband's inability to tap into his memory bank and deal with the open wounds that were oozing poison into his thought life was destroying the very fragments of his marriage. The husband, a victim of what I term occasional knots (moments that cause trauma and lifelong damage to one's personality) was additionally a victim of foundational knots (childhood family dysfunction). Just like the wife, he had also grown up in dysfunction yet had been given the role of the man of his household whilst never having witnessed the role of the "man of the house" modelled.

So, what do we have here? We have a wife and

a husband, a mother and a father to four young children who have never seen successful parenthood or marriage modelled. A wife, whose fear of losing the family that she had always wanted was causing her to hold on so tight that her grip had become suffocating to her mate. A husband, who has no idea what it is to be a man through lack of fatherhood and whose inability to tap into the wounds of his childhood was holding him back from manhood and keeping him bound, knots that were being played out in infidelity and a lack of family structure.

What a shame it is that we all attend weddings in our best attire and throw confetti, we even have social media hashtags for the big occasion, but no one takes a moment to truly pray the couple out of the bondage of their past that could lead them to divorce, and worse still, further soulish destruction tomorrow. I put it to you that love (our human perception of strong emotional attachment and affection for another) is no reason enough to celebrate marriage. We must begin to strive towards two unknotted, whole people joining together to create an indeed holy matrimony.

Flaws and all

As the Lord began to lead me down this journey and revelation of the concept of the unknotting, one thing I realised when it came to marriage was how knots attracted knots. I became more conscience to the marriages around me and witnessed how one person's dysfunction was the soothing balm to another's and vice versa. A dangerous game indeed. I witnessed marriages that contained a wife with major daddy issues marry a man with severe mummy issues, or a husband desperate not to be like daddy find himself a wife avoiding being like mummy at all cost. Or worse still a man dealing with the issue of validation bag himself a stunner of a wife as his "prize" or certification of manhood and a wife unaware of her self-worth being perfectly ok with subconsciously being a man's trophy. The two found one another and believed they were loving *despite* their flaws, failing to realise that they were loving *because* of their flaws. They had become subconsciously attracted to one another's weaknesses and not strengths, they had found what I term a *knot mate*, someone just as damaged as they were and their invisible dysfunction became a safe haven.

> One person's dysfunction was the soothing balm to another's.

I remember once seeing a guy that had what I call the knight in shining armour syndrome. He had knots that meant he suffered from a lack of identity and the need to feel like the saviour in whatever environment he was in, and there I was, a girl with undetected daddy issues who desperately wanted to be loved and saved. The "saviour" came in contact with one that desperately needed saving. It's safe to say you can imagine how that little spell of romance ended. Do you see how one's dysfunction can attract another's? How many marriage ceremonies have you attended and thrown your best suit or dress on for, celebrating a couple that have fallen for one another's knots and became more entangled in the ropes of life after they had promised "I do"?

Internal marital dysfunction

For children starved of love and affection in their home as a child, growing up to be transparent adults can be the hardest task of all. For many, living closed has become a way of life and the idea of opening up to another is nothing short of impossible. This often sees marriages that are open to a degree but closed enough to still protect one's own self. A way of living that will crush any martial union. The very essence of marriage demands complete transparency and total openness, but how can one be open and transparent with another when they haven't first learnt to be open with themselves? In my example above the husband protested to his wife that he hadn't

> *The very essence of marriage demands complete transparency and total openness.*

even told himself this big secret that hung over his life and was affecting his emotions and ultimately determining his behaviour patterns, yet he remained in a union that demanded complete and total transparency.

False Intimacy

Other traits that can follow us into our own marriages, when coming from a background of witnessing a dysfunctional marriage and not having a positive model of a biblical home, includes settling for false intimacy. When we are not aware of what true love looks like, we can believe the lie that physical contact or words as sweet as honey alone equate love. We have never seen sacrificial love, a love that is patient and kind nor a love which keeps no record of wrongs, we simply settle for that which *feels* like love.

It is also possible that we go on to deal with false expectations of what we perceive a marital union to be over what it *actually* is. We may face dealing with a spirit of Jezebel (a spirit which aims to manipulate, control and in turn dominate its subject) in order to have things our own way in a home. Of course, those coming from the perfect 2.0 family home can also find themselves dealing with these issues, but I'd say suffering dysfunction within our family homes as children makes us more at risk of such traits.

Going on to have our own families and introduce children into the mix of such dysfunctional patterns that lie in our thinking and our viewpoint of life does of course mean we take the chance of continuing on such dysfunctional patterns in our generations to come.

However, are we doomed in marriages and raising families because we failed to see one modelled? The answer is of course no, not when we invite Christ into the picture. As you read on, you'll find tools to freedom which include dealing with rejection, handling memories and breaking patterns.

6

DYSFUNCTIONAL BEHAVIOURS

A natural by-product of dysfunctional foundations is often dysfunctional behaviour. That is behaviour that does us no good but one which we can't seem to separate ourselves from. It is essentially self-destructive or self-soothing reactions or end results to the culture of brokenness in which many of us have been reared.

Have you ever met someone and wondered why they are the way they are? Why they behave the way in which they do? Why they are so self-destructive, so insecure, riddled with low self-esteem, painfully clingy or worse still, violent, full of anger, driven by rage or cold in personality and unable to feel? This chapter may help you to see and understand that individual or possibly yourself better.

I liken dysfunctional behaviour to a baby in a crib. Unable to vocalise their need, a baby wails in its attempt to gain the attention of those that it believes have access to provide them with their need. With no affordable means of communication between the adult and baby realm, those surrounding the child are left to do a guess work in their bid to sooth the child, often times, giving the baby, not want it actually desired or craved, but whatever *they* could find to *silence* the loud cries of the disturbed or disturbing child with soothing items often being a pacifier or a favourite toy.

{ *A natural by-product of dysfunctional foundations is often dysfunctional behaviour.* }

When it comes to the link between dysfunctional foundations and dysfunctional behaviours, I highlight in this moment that *we* are both the child and the adult in the above scenario. The baby in my example above is our soul, and the adult is our physical being. With our soul unable to communicate, "this is where it hurts"; yet aware of its pain, it cries out continuously in its bid to gain some form of comfort to its brokenness. Our adult self, unable to cope with the loud sounds of pain from our soul, finds a quick fix, be it a pacifier, a toy, a blanket, also known as, pornography, drugs, men, sex, keeping busy, degrees, women, fast cars, career, money, gambling, violence, stealing, shopping, over eating, over working, social media, chasing titles, fame... and the list of course becomes endless, in order to silence the unbearable cries of a hurting soul.

With our soul in pain and crying out for a mending to its broken state, our physical self does what it knows, it uses what is within reach and finds what is easy and accessible in order to fix the cry. The only issue here is, if we are to use the above example, when a child has a deeper medical issue and continues to cry, pacifiers and toys may work for a moment, but of course the cries continue and often come back louder and stronger until the child is taken for medical attention when it is perceived something more serious could be taking place.

I'm reminded of times on public transport or when flying to another country. Often times, there will be a crying baby on a flight or a train. Full of irritation and annoyance at the sounds of the crying child other passengers will often give deadly stares to the adult carrying the child with a gentle "shut that child up" stance. When our soul cries out for mending, society is also often quick to ask that we do whatever is needed to perform a quick fix. In our bid to hide our brokenness from an irritated world and those around us, we do just that, we shut our soul up by providing quick fixes which will eventually lead to further brokenness down the line.

Life for me can be an interesting one. Often times, I may come across someone with a clear ache in their soul. Seeing the outworking of their brokenness sometimes portrayed in traits such as a clingy nature or fear, I can either decide in that moment to tend to the ache or simply give it a quick fix. I have found that prayer can at times be a quick fix, knowing that someone's soul is aching I can decide on a quick *"God bless you and keep you"* or I can do what I ought to do, which is to take my time to sit down with this individual, counsel them through and see to where it hurts.

> *Prayer can at times be a quick fix.*

Roots and fruits

In keeping with my study when putting together this book, I began to find that no tree just produces bad fruit. There is ultimately a root to every fruit that we find and to every badly perceived soul there are reasons to their dysfunction. I have chosen the person of Gomer in the Bible in which to exemplify this through.

A study of Gomer

In the book of Hosea, we see a prophet asked of the

Lord to marry a prostitute named Gomer. One would have thought Gomer to have been thankful that, considering her state as a sinful woman, she was to be taken in by a great man of the Lord. Gomer however, though married to Hosea, continues her lifestyle of promiscuity, sleeping with other men and having children by them. Hosea continuously takes her back, a wonderful picture of our Lord's redemptive power and grace towards Israel and more so His own bride. Considering Gomer's behaviour, it would be easy to consider her an ungrateful sinner; it would be wise however, to take a look into why she was doing that which she did.

Though the only source of roots that could be found, Gomer's family name is indication enough of her coming from a tainted past. We learn that Gomer was born of Diblaim, a name meaning double layer, indicating that sexual sin ran throughout this bloodline. Is it any surprise that Gomer would end up a harlot? Her fruit was simply a result of her roots.

Now looking into the 21st century, some of the fruits that we find as a result of the roots of dysfunction I discuss below.

In March of 2017, the ministry that I am blessed to steward, Pure Hearts, ran a counselling course which saw young women come for 8 weeks of emotional and mental freedom. Using the truth of the word of God, we dug up issues that some of these millennial women were facing. Issues in the room ranged from eating disorders to severe anger and rage or drug use. With the knowledge that dysfunctional behaviour is no more than physical manifestations of dysfunctional roots we searched deeper for the root of these issues. On our search, we found that beneath eating disorders, drug use, and anger or rage was parental disappointment, incest / sexual abuse and divorced parents just to name a few.

> Dysfunctional behaviour is no more than physical manifestations of dysfunctional roots.

Other forms of dysfunctional behaviours can and often do include character traits such as an overactive fearful imagination, nail biting, cutting, an unkept appearance (e.g. hair or nails), excessive lying, excessive eating, excessive spending and overall self-abuse. I am certain many of us have been, currently are, or know of some individuals with one or some of these traits. I challenge you to look beyond the dysfunction and consider the why.

In our world today, I am so saddened to see that social media is encouraging dysfunctional behaviour. For the one already plagued with rejection, platforms built around comparison by encouraging a lifestyle of well filtered photos to gain the approval of others, a showing of ones perfectly toned abs or bought curves or borrowed fast cars and designer items in order to gain the approval of others is further enhancing their dysfunction. We have become a society of dysfunctional people crying out for acceptance from one another.

Dysfunctional behaviour can also show up in the form of what is *not* done, though it is often only thought of as behaviour that is outwardly exhibited. Did you know that you can suffer from dysfunction through what you fail to do? I remember being so afraid of confrontation that if I went for a service and was given a less than professional service or a totally different outcome than I desired (e.g. at the hairdressers) I would leave without a saying a word. Not because I was a pleasant God-fearing peacekeeper, but because I was petrified of confrontation. Confrontation to me meant the recipient to the voicing of my concerns or displeasure would no longer like me. You see I wanted to be liked so much so that I sacrificed the truth in order to be accepted. I allowed myself to be walked over and treated less than my value or getting my money's worth because I preferred to be liked.

> We have become a society of dysfunctional people crying out for acceptance from one another.

I remember a time that I went to a salon and

asked for a new hairstyle with bangs. I was certain that I wanted to use a weave to achieve this style but my stylist convinced me to mix in my own hair to achieve a fuller look, which meant cutting my own hair a considerably huge amount. In a bid to comply, to be liked and to be seen as bold and unafraid, I agreed. I would like to take this time to say this; if you are a black woman like I am or are familiar with black women like I, you'll be aware that *it is real in these streets* for us and length does not happen overnight. To allow a stylist to literally chop away at my hair for the sake of achieving bangs was nothing short of crazy, simply because it wasn't what I wanted, but I allowed it. And the story gets worse. She completed the look and to my horror it looked horrific. I smiled. I paid. I thanked her. And I left. I walked into Iceland to buy some frozen foods on my way home and the man serving me at the till didn't look me in the eye, *he looked me in the bangs*. I knew what he was thinking, and he knew that I knew what he was thinking. I took my change and I left the store. I entered my house, grabbed a scissor and that hairstyle was no more. Hilarious, I know! However, the true point to highlight here is a level of dysfunction that would cause one to be so afraid to speak up in fear of not being liked. The idea of allowing another person to make decisions on your life without your joyful agreement simply because you fear their rejection.

Now you may consider the inability to speak up to be a childlike trait and one that may be grown out of, but in actual fact desiring to be liked so much so that one fails to be vocal about the truth is a clear sign of a lack of identity. When a person is secure in their identity, in who they are and mainly in Whose they are, they become unafraid of confrontation and come to understand it as healthy. They find no fear in vocalising their likes and dislikes in anticipation of the disapproval of others.

I would like to help you to spot dysfunctional behaviour patterns in your own life should you be dealing with any such a trait.

Living for reactions

A sign of dysfunction is when a person performs, speaks or makes decisions driven by the desire to gain approval from others. When you pick the type of car that you will drive, the place you will live, the clothes you wear or the way in which you portray yourself to the world in a bid to gain approval from the world, this is a clear sign of dysfunction being an underlying problem.

A possessive nature

When one gets close to another, be it a spouse, a friend or a group of people and finds themselves incredibly fearful of losing this individual when moments of natural separations occur, this is again another clear sign of dysfunction, a sign of one unable to function independently of others and requires an intimately close relationship in order to find self-worth and value. For a male, this could be an unhealthy control issue with a spouse or potential spouse, for a female it could be a refusal to let go even when made clear that a particular man is not for you.

Social awkwardness

On the best of days each of us can find it difficult to interact with and be confident in the environment of new faces or indeed old ones. Social awkwardness, however, goes deeper than this. It is an absolute fear of being seen, being heard and a preference to shy away from the crowd. It is when one makes decisions about their life in an effort to avoid moments of social interaction. Such a trait of dysfunction may have come from moments of trauma, a lack of celebration of one's personality in a household, or worse still, a mockery of it.

Condemnation

Condemnation is defined as strong disapproval of a thing or person. To feel condemned is often to feel that one has done something wrong, is behaving wrong or speaking wrong. I once met a young man whose mother policed him and his brothers eating as a child. As he ate amongst friends and family she would scold him for the manner in which he ate or the way that he chewed. She did this constantly throughout his childhood. He grew up to be a very self-conscience and self-aware in the area of food, leading to an eating disorder in later life. By his mother's disapproval of him he grew up believing that he was disapproved of. He grew up always feeling condemned. Condemnation is a trait of dysfunctional behaviour which many of us struggle with, the feeling of being disapproved of, without actually having done anything wrong, can be the underlying root to much of our day to day issues.

Transferred fears

I used to be incredibly afraid of dogs, to be honest I still am extremely weary of anything that moves that isn't human. The fear became so overwhelming at one time that I asked the Lord, *"where did this fear come from?"* He responded, *"your mother"*. I continued to speak to the Lord about this and He showed me the following. Growing up in a household where animals are feared and not celebrated, as a child if a dog came anywhere near me I was pulled away very quickly and we spent our childhood being told to avoid animals because they were dangerous. In actual fact, dogs (in their majority) are not dangerous at all, but I was taught to fear them because my parent/s feared them. This fear wasn't actually mine, but a generational fear that was passed unto me. As children, we often view the world out of the eye of the one that raised us. If we are told to fear dogs, we grow believing them to be dangerous creatures, but if we are taught to touch and stroke dogs, we grow up believing them to be loving beings. Many thought patterns, fears or behaviours are often transferred to us, continuing cycles of dysfunction.

> Many thought patterns, fears or behaviours are often transferred to us, continuing cycles of dysfunction.

Dysfunctional behaviour in and of itself is a thief. It robs the individual of their true self. For example, the one dealing with social awkwardness may actually be a fantastic orator and communicator; I, shockingly, may actually be an incredible dog lover, but such a trait of dysfunction rooted in childhood trauma, learnt behaviour or broken foundations continues to mask true identity. The one clinging on to another for dear life out of fear of losing a lover or friend robs themselves of the opportunity to discover the greatness within their own self. And lastly the one living for the reaction or approval of others has never experienced the peace that comes with not needing to please or impress anyone but the Lord.

Breaking free – what's your why?

Breaking free of dysfunctional behaviours takes a root searching. For much of this book you have learnt about paternal ties, maternal ties, behaviours and family breakdowns; in order to become free of dysfunctional behaviour knowing your *why* is key. It is important that you realise the root to your particular dysfunctional or self-destructive behaviour. Firstly, identify your dysfunctional behaviour and then ask yourself what is missing that you are attempting to fill? What cry is your soul wailing, what scars lie within from childhood and what false comforts are you using to sooth the ache? You may even do well to ask yourself what positions have you taken up in life to fill your insecurity. I once heard a teacher of the word state that, *"the pulpit is the worse place for the insecure"*. His point was this, for the one dealing with insecurity or inadequacy the applause of the people becomes a soothing balm, but as we discussed earlier this will be nothing more than a temporary fix. Some of us have taken up positions, chased degrees and taken up career titles or started businesses, not out of obedience to the Lord or even a following of passion, but simply to boost our feeling of adequacy. For some, we perceive our importance and relevance based on what we do and not on who we are, a glaringly clear sign of a lack of identity.

When considering temporary fixes, a scary thought is that they actually work! Void fillers are great because they do actually cure the ache, but for a moment. The men, the sex, the drugs, the pornography, the applause of men are great void fillers. They make us feel good and ease the ache in the soul temporarily. When a soul finds a filler that works and works instantly and well, guess what it does? It continues to return to that place, it continues to need the filler, creating the giant of addiction. Drug addition, sex addiction, food addiction, pornography addiction and the like are interesting void fillers because they work so well and quickly. Jesus met with a woman at a well in John 4 and identified her lust problem and her love of men in order to fill her void. He made mention of the amount of men that she had gotten through in her search for love and then explained that through drinking from these "wells" she continued to thirst. This is the same as our void fillers today. We may indeed receive comfort from them, but the comfort will last only but a moment and we must keep coming back to them (a cycle of addiction and self-destruction). Jesus invites this woman to drink from Himself, the well of living water. He introduces her to a cup of water that she would only need to drink once yet find fulfilment for a lifetime.

> We perceive our importance and relevance based on what we do and not on who we are, a glaringly clear sign of a lack of identity.

When you and I come to the Lord and allow ourselves to break the pattern of using void fillers, but instead go to the Lord and ask that He show us the roots of our pain, we can begin the process of true healing and not settle for momentary fixes.

So, young lady I guarantee you, you are not a clingy insecure mess, there is a root to your dysfunction. And young man, you are not full of anger and rage, something is broken within and your soul is crying out for mending. You can find the healing you require when you decide to give up the patterns of dysfunctional behaviour that you have allowed to plague your day to day life.

SECTION 3:
FINDING FREEDOM

7

THE ROOT OF REJECTION

A word that has been frequently used in our world today is the word, 'rejection'. What we consider a slight everyday happening is actually often at the root of much our dysfunction. Rejection, if you like, is the unseen driving force behind much of our behaviour, actions and choices as adult beings. Much of the rejection that we faced as a child (whether through a father's absence or a mother's abuse) continue to plague our subconscious mind causing us to act out in the natural. Rejection, we can say, is the wind beneath the wings of dysfunctional behaviour patterns. If you have identified forms of dysfunctional behaviour in your life but have struggled to pinpoint what the actual problem or root is, you may do well to consider rejection as your diagnosis.

Though a word that we (the church) tend to use often as a diagnosis of issues, I am not sure we quite understand the severity and plethora of problems that a root cause of rejection can cause in one's life. Though we may all suffer moments of rejection in life, for example, a man may feel rejected when attempting to talk to a female who gives him zero time of play, or a woman may feel rejected when her girlfriends have a girl's night out without her, these are moments of rejection that any human being is bound to feel. However, a deep root of rejection suggests rejection that has embedded itself within a person's soul and has become the driving force or stumbling block behind much of their life's decisions or inaction. Rejection can cause a person to take opportunities that were never meant for them, or on the other hand, cause another to avoid opportunities that were perfectly suited to them.

The Oxford Dictionary describes rejection as *a refusal to accept a person or thing and (or) to throw away or discard*. When we experience rejection in our early years or family set up, this is, in essence, the message that is sent to our soul (our mind, will and emotions); that we are not accepted, not fit for use, easy to throw away or discard. I know of a lady whose mother passed away at the age of eight. Following such a traumatic event most children would be surrounded by much love and as much care as possible would be taken to ensure their day to day structure is affected as little as possible. Unfortunately, this was not the case. Though her siblings were well taken care of, she endured the incredibly rejecting experience of "who will take her in?" such a rejection is dire to one's soul and traits of which cannot help but seep (I'd go as far as to say attempt to plague) our adult life.

Rejection can find its introduction into our lives through different channels, or what I consider, open doors. Family is of course the starting point. As the institution called to nurture, instruct and raise us, one of the fundamental roles of the family is to ensure that a child feels secure, wanted and loved. To fail in providing these key ingredients to a child during their formative or teenage years is to leave them wide open to rejection. When our fathers leave the home and fail to return, or set up home elsewhere with children just like us but that are not us, this sends a message to a child of, *"you are not worth my staying"*. When a mother fails to emotionally nurture and carefully carve out time of love and affection for a child, again, it sends messages to a child of, *"you are not worth loving"*. Though as adults, we can see in hindsight that the issue here of course is

> One of the fundamental roles of the family is to ensure that a child feels secure, wanted and loved.

not the child but the adults in question, a child's mind is not yet broad or filled with enough knowledge or understanding to yet grasp this truth. Children can only see and understand that, *"something must be wrong with me"*. Though the words may not leave their mouth, the lie reaches their heart.

Rejection as a child can also take place through peers, the education system and sibling rivalry. Joseph was of course loved by his father but rejected by his own brothers and sold into slavery. Joseph's source of rejection therefore may not have come from his parents but it still did come from within his own household through his siblings.

The education system may play a part in rejection simply based on its set up. The system, designed to celebrate those whose abilities align with its structure, can cause children without the natural ability to add and subtract but more favoured in baking and gymnastics or the like of creativity to feel, *"something is wrong with me, I am not smart"*. With such a self-label already impressed upon a child's mind, many enter into adulthood with the same mentality, often fearing moments that demand intellectual ability in day to day life or the work place. Such an early label coming from hierarchy of intelligence causes a child to feel rejected from the norm and to view themselves as easily discarded or of not as great in importance as the highest test scorer in the classroom.

Unmet expectations

Rejection is often always found in places of unmet expectations. No child desires that their life fails to meet up to their parents' expectation. There are some tribes in Africa where a baby boy, as a first born, is the expectation of not only the father but the entire family, friends and tribe. At one time, when a woman would birth a female as her firstborn child such disappointment would hit her and she would feel as though she had failed in her duty of baby production. Rejection as a means of failed expectation can go as far as the happenings in the Karo village in Ethiopia where babies were thrown and fed to crocodiles if they were born twins, had their top teeth grow first or were considered illegitimate. These children were rejected because they failed to meet the deception of thought pattern in a village which stated that only children with bottom teeth that grew first, not twins and born into a perfect family structure, were fit for use.

> *Rejection is often always found in places of unmet expectations.*

Again, rejection can come in the form of feeling like one's life failed to measure up to *"what my parents wanted for me"*. In some African cultures, to have a child unable to graduate from university is considered nothing short of a shame to the family. I met a lady once whose family were fair in complexion and all of the children followed suit. That is of course until she was born almost as dark as night with the most beautiful chocolate skin. Of course, her family didn't see it as beautiful, they saw her as odd and were perplexed by her shade often making it a reference point for comedy; she failed to meet the family's expectation of how children in this particular home were to look. All of these forms of rejection based on expectations, of course false expectations, can damage a child's view of themselves and cause one to feel unfit for use, easily discarded and unwanted.

Effects of rejection

Though rejection in of itself is painful enough, the effects of rejection are more costly. To be rejected on such a deep level by ones' own family can cause what we term, fear of rejection. Fear of rejection is the idea that once a person has been burnt in a particular way they will often always fear being hurt in that same manner again. Recently, the world watched on as Grenfell Tower in London burnt for almost 24 hours with families, babies

> *Though rejection in of itself is painful enough, the effects of rejection are more costly.*

and the elderly trapped within the high-rise building. Some managed to escape the real-life inferno whilst battling for every breath. However, their survival is of course plagued by daily torment. I can only imagine that the next time they saw smoke, on any level, it triggered memories of the moment they were trapped in the fire, I can imagine they no longer ever want to live in a high-rise building, I am almost certain sound sleep may be a privilege of the past. This is the same with fear of rejection. Though the situation, event or circumstances may be over, we continue to feel the effects of it as adults, we subconsciously fear it happening again in a different way.

Fear of rejection causes us to have a fight or flight mentality. If we spent most of our lives suffering rejection, or having been rejected, it causes us as adults to prepare to be rejected again. Our soul says something like this, "*Ill reject them before they reject me*". This mentality causes us to push away situations and people who at times have caused us no harm or meant no harm in their genuine mistake toward us, but the fear of being rejected again caused us to act first before we got hurt again.

For God hath not given us the spirit of fear; but of power, and of love, and of a sound mind. (2 Timothy 1:7)

I believe we have grown so accustomed to words such as fear and rejection that we have forgotten the key component of 2 Timothy 1:7 which is the word, *spirit*. Just as fear is a spirit (a personality without a body), so is rejection. God reminds us that He has not given us such a personality or character trait. That is to say, rejection carries with it a personality. There is a personality type to rejection, and it is glaringly obvious to the trained eye when rejection plagues the life of an individual. In my first book, *The Delivery Room*, I speak on the different types of rejection personalities that we may see. I expand on these below.

> *Rejection carries with it a personality.*

Though rejection can affect us all, the effects of rejection in our lives can often play themselves out in different ways. Some of us are so affected by rejection that we dare not step outside the parameters of perceived safety that we have created for ourselves. We cannot fathom how we will interact with new people, how we will behave in a foreign environment and certainly cannot imagine ourselves bold and confident in the midst of strangers. Rejection causes us to stay safe only in the areas which we have grown accustomed to, ultimately causing us to miss out on a fulfilled life. Whilst on the other hand, some are affected by rejection through being fuelled by an obsessive level of ambition. Unhealthy ambition can cause one to people please, to live filled with a desire to have a life that *looks* good though it be rotting away on the inside. This of course leads me unto my next point, those that are so wounded by rejection but nurse their sores in private. Rejection sufferers like these often carry much bravado, the idea of putting on one face to the world but hiding their fears and deeply crippling rejection. Such a trait is of course a dangerous one as it often leads one to their own self-destruction. Though hurting beyond a level of pain they are able to withstand, the idea of looking weak or vulnerable is a far more frightening thought.

Rejection of course can be more sinister in its effects. It can cause some of us to live a life of, "*I don't need anybody*", a thought pattern which often always proves invalid. I once watched a documentary, I believe it was titled something along the lines of, *the naked truth of the porn industry*. A seasoned porn star who had now left the industry shared how her desire for porn was fuelled by her desire not to rely on anybody else for finances. She shared how her father had kicked her out of her family home as a young woman; approached by a stranger on the street who promised her $40 for her to perform sexual favours for men that were waiting in an apartment a few streets away, she took the opportunity over having to return home to beg a father who had thrown her out on the street. She went on to share how following each scene that she would participate in, she would cry private tears of shame as the camera crew and the room full of men prepared to move unto the next. I watched this woman share her story with brokenness in my heart for her. I saw a woman who did not want the lifestyle that she enrolled herself to, but plagued with rejection from her own father she found herself wanting to fend for herself financially and possibly seeking love from a source unable to provide her with even an ounce of it.

Seeking a replacement of where we were rejected is often another character trait that is seen with those who have a root of dysfunction related to rejection. When we are rejected, especially in our childhood, it is as though we walk around with a gaping hole within. We see from the science of the body that the natural human makeup is to mend where is wounded or broken. Should we suffer a cut, the body kicks in the operation of healing and mending the broken place by eventually creating new skin to over the wound. Our soul attempts the same mending. When our soul is broken by rejection or left with an exposed wound, our soul attempts to find a remedy to the brokenness. The only issue here is, when the body repairs the body, it has the correct parts to mend with, but the soul cannot possibly mend itself, as it does not have the parts to mend with, only the lover of soul, Christ Jesus, has the correct missing parts that are needed to do a complete work in making us whole. However, without this knowledge, the human soul (often the mind) begins the process of searching for a replacement to sooth our pain. Depending on the gender of the individual, this attempt to heal can take on different forms.

For females that have suffered rejection, especially that related to fatherhood, a desire and almost unhealthy obsession for male attention, marriage and a love story could be the soul's remedy. Other forms of a remedy could be placing a huge amount of attention on one's physical appearance in a bid to cover up the internal brokenness. Self-consciousness and insecurity often follow this and a large character trait would be overdoing and an overall clingy nature. When a soul has been rejected it can fear rejection again so strongly that it clings on to anything that looks like love and affection and becomes petrified at the thought of losing it. This is why many females who have suffered greatly from rejection may feel there was or is a man that they are crazy in love with (a feeling that is not reciprocated by the male in question) when in actual fact their soul is simply holding on dearly to this individual in a desire not to feel the pains of rejection once again.

For a male, the out workings of rejection can differ. Whilst a rejected female may cling unto one individual for dear life, a rejected male may play the field with multiple women in a bid to prove he was always worth acceptance. The soul may find its remedy in knowing, *"see, you are loved and wanted, look at the vast number of women that want you"*. A statement which, in reality, does nothing to smooth over the damage or wounds of the soul, especially when caused by a father walking out or a mother emotionally absent and a little boy that was starved of love and affirmation.

For both genders, the result of roots of dysfunction can birth fruits such as anger. An emotion of the body which often comes to fruition at the soul's highest level of pain and frustration. Where the little boy or the little girl cannot speak, the man or woman lashes out with fits of rage. When children that have endured childhood rejection go on to enter into relationships or marriages without first truly dealing with the roots of their dysfunction, their partners, new families and children are unfortunately often the recipients of their anger. The wife or husband of such a man or woman can often wonder, *"why is he or she so easily angered"* they can see the fruit, but cannot perceive the root.

Where the little boy or the little girl cannot speak, the man or woman lashes out with fits of rage.

21st century diseases, such as anxiety and social disorders, can also be linked back to a childhood root of rejection. I once had a friend when I was 17 years old who was crippled with anxiety. Though undiagnosed, it was clear that the thoughts that sat in her mind were playing themselves out in her day to day life. At that time, I believe social media had just gained strong popularity amongst the teens, we would sit in the school playground and take endless group pictures to upload unto our various social media accounts. I recall a couple of times where she was asked to take a picture of the group. Whilst we all held our smiles and waited patiently for her to press the button, the silence was deafening. We watched on as her hands would shake ever so nervously as fear gripped her mind in the moment. Months later I was able to pray with her and conversation led to talks of her childhood. She shared with me how her father was violent and mean spirited in the home, she was afraid to speak and move in fear of a backlash. The shakes and level of fear when asked to take centre stage and lead a group photo now made perfect sense. When one is used to fear and the feeling of being afraid such a daily lifestyle can cause severe anxiousness and a state of unrest.

Being the result of a spirit at work (the *spirit* of rejection) rejection can do one of three things:

1. Affect our hearing

When a soul has been greatly affected by rejection it is possible that they begin to hear things that were simply not said. For example, should it be that a spouse desires to spend time alone and requests this of their partner, a partner with a root of rejection could hear, *"I don't want to spend time with you, you are starting to annoy or frustrate me, I don't love you anymore"*. Though very far from what was communicated, rejection can cause us to hear others through the funnel of our root of rejection and not the reality of the truth.

2. Affect our sight

Rejection can also cause one to see life through the lenses of our pain. We can begin to see that no one loves us, people don't want us around, the world is better without us in it, this person is preferred above me, all of which of course are incredibly far from the truth. Rejection can be likened to wearing tinted glasses, everything appears dark and gloomy until we take them off. For some, it could be rose gold glasses, where the spirit of rejection causes them to over arch their own self-importance and no one matters in their world except them, the soul's remedy to their feelings of a lack of importance as a child.

3. Affect our sensitivity

Rejection can affect our sensitivity by heightening our emotions. It can overplay the words of another to us and cause us to feel that we were severely attacked and done a wrong when we may have been rightly corrected. Rejection causes a soul to be overly sensitive to criticism. It says, *"when you criticise or correct me, I feel like I'm not fit for use again, I'm easily discarded once again and not accepted as I am"*. For this particular character trait of rejection, it makes it incredibly hard for one to become better. In order to grow, we need criticism, we require chastening and sharpening, but when the root of rejection acts as a road block we are unable to receive the correct nutrients of discipline to grow.

For alot of us rejection does and continues to play a huge role in our day to day lives leading us to continue to live malfunctioning. We cannot live our best life nor be our best self when we are plagued with the root of rejection.

"Before I formed thee in the belly I knew thee" (Jeremiah 1:5, extracted)

For the one dealing with rejection at its roots so deep that it has and continues to plague day to day life and interactions, relationships and possibly even your mental state, it is important to know that the circumstances that brought about the feelings or character traits of rejection were a terrible wrong that occurred, they are situations that shouldn't have happened; however, they are situations that you can overcome. As discussed above, the soul in its remedy attempts to go back to the source of rejection and seeks its' own healing by finding a replica to what wasn't provided. If it was a daddy issue it may attempt to replace it with male attention, if it was a lack of motherly love, it may attempt to have multiple children of its own to love and mother, none of which will ever satisfy the brokenness that was caused or sooth the wounds that run so deep. Our only option with the Lord is to exchange our perspective for His.

> *Our only option with the Lord is to exchange our perspective for His.*

The start of Jeremiah 1:5 sees the Lord declare to Jeremiah that before He formed him in his mother's womb, He knew him. That is a comforting thought and the greatest healer to rejection. When rejection shouts, *"you are unlovable, you are unwanted, and uncared for"*, the Lord has spoken, *"you are known"*. This declaration to Jeremiah allows us insight to the following...

> *When rejection shouts, "you are unlovable, you are unwanted, and uncared for", the Lord has spoken, "you are known".*

You are not an accident

One of the greatest lies of rejection to an individual is that they don't belong here. Rejection whispers in a person's ear (often confirmed by the circumstances of their birth) that they are simply a number or an accident unplanned by their parents. Jeremiah 1:5 however, lets us know that we were not an accident, we were a thought in the Lord's mind long before our parents ever knew about our existence.

You were carefully designed

Rejection linked to physicality that says, *"I'm too dark, too light, too tall, too short,"* loses the power of its deception when we believe Jeremiah 1:5. The Lord declares to Jeremiah that He formed him in his mother's womb. The word, 'form', is to bring together and create something. The Lord brought all the pieces of you together, He chose the right ears, the right nose and eyes and skin tone perfect for your design.

You are known

The most common lie that rejection spews to a person is, *"no one understands me"*. Again, an untruth that is trumped by the Lord's simple words to Jeremiah, *"I knew you"*. Before He ever manifested our being here on earth the Lord knew us and set us apart for His good pleasure.

In our bid to uproot the root of rejection which plagues our life with dysfunction, we must meditate on this truth, we are not an accident, we are carefully designed and fully known and understood by our maker.

8

PILGRIM OF MEMORIES

When it comes to dysfunction and family/generational dysfunction, one of the roots that cause us to stay stuck is our inability to forget the past. Whilst the Christian faith encourages forgiveness and not harbouring bitterness, we fail to deal with the biggest thing that causes many to stay stuck and unable to move past their dysfunction; memories.

In His absolute sovereignty God created human beings with the ability to remember. Our cognitive ability allows us to remember God's goodness, to remember who we are, our name, our families, where we live and so much more. We *need* our memory. The essence of memory is mentioned greatly in the word of God as a means to purposeful and effective living. David was able to defeat Goliath fuelled by his memory of when God had previously helped him defeat a lion, Job was able to stay the course of his suffering by remembering the times when God had been good to him in the past, the children of Israel were encouraged to remember the God that led their ancestors through the wilderness in a bid to hold on to His faithfulness, they created stones of *memorials* to help them to *remember* and Abraham trusted God whenever He *remembered* the faithful God that gave him a son in his infertile age.

Memories can be sources of good thoughts and can propel us to a great future when we remember the pleasures of the past and consider the joys that could lie ahead. Our ability to remember is also a great indication of our resemblance to our creator; God. Our God is one with the ability to remember.

> *For I will be merciful to their unrighteousness, and their sins and their iniquities will I remember no more. (Hebrews 8:12)*

In order for God to provide mercy, He must make the choice to remember an aspect of our nature or sin no more. You and I, in order to move forward in life and truly become unknotted, must also decide to remember some things and situations no more. However, this becomes difficult when the enemy of our soul uses negative memories as a means to keep us bound. For many of us, memories of a violent home, shouting matches between parents, abuse, being bullied, neglect and utter dysfunction are visuals that plague our mind, ultimately causing us to think negatively and subsequently affecting our day to day lives, especially our personalities and social attributes as human beings. Some of us find it difficult to enter our family homes as sad or negative memories saturate our very being the moment we walk through our front door. I call memories "timeless moments" that reside in our minds and each time we remember that thing, person or moment it is as though we are right back in the very *time* the event occurred. Memories can be toxic and stop us from moving forward. A wife attempting to overcome her husband's infidelity could be doing well in their marriage and process to restoration until she *remembers* how unfaithful her husband was to her. Whilst positive memories can act as slingshots to propel us forward and give us a boost of faith into exploring newness, I liken negative memories to a rubber band being tied around a person's waist. The band becomes caught on the door knob and no matter how far the person gets away from the door, just one trigger of that memory and the person is pulled right back to the door (memory). With negative memories therefore, one can only get so far, but eventually will be pulled back to the dysfunction of their past.

Memories are triggers

As shared in a previous chapter, I remember once running up the communal stairs of my childhood home, filled with the thoughts of imminent violence I ran up the stairs in a bid to stop my parents from arguing, their shouts I could hear from the ground floor and I sprinted my way up to the 3rd floor apartment, falling flat on my face half way through the race but failing to let that deter me. I rushed into our flat and dashed into the kitchen to find my mother cooking stew, home alone. To my amazement, there was no fight because my father wasn't there, my mind had tricked me into believing I had heard sounds of violent fighting which didn't really exist in that moment. In this instance, I had heard an isolated noise that triggered my mind to wonder into my memory bank and pick out the memory of my parents fighting. Such a terrifying memory sent signals to my brain and caused me to cease up in fear and in that single moment I lost all rational and nothing could be truer to me at that time than the truth of what I believed in my head. It wasn't until I saw my mother in the kitchen alone (I believe humming a tune or other) and cooking stew in the lovely summer's afternoon that I knew my thoughts to have been a lie.

The personal prison of memories

What shocks me when writing about this is that if I were to ask my mother about this moment she would struggle to remember it, I'm pretty sure she will have zero recollection of it all together. She may not be able to remember other moments of arguing also. But I sure can remember it. You see, *I* can remember these moments because they were moments that greatly affected me, but for those that were not so affected, it was a fleeting happening in a day's events. Memories can be personal prisons for us, especially as children. When we see the world from a child's perspective everything looks bigger and grander than it actually is. I still recall always believing my dad was the tallest man in the world at 5"10, as a child he just appeared huge to me. This can be the same with our memories as events, moments of trauma and anger or violence are remembered not as big or as bad as they actually were, but as big or bad as we *perceived* them to be. Memories can also be magnified based on the limited information that we have. Children suffering the trauma of seeing a dead body, for example, can be scarred with this imprint image in their minds for numerous years and well into their adulthood. Most children don't understand the concept of death, the assuredness of life coming to an end or what happens when a person dies. To witness a lifeless body therefore (especially that of someone they knew well), not only causes incredible fear but creates utter devastation and confusion.

> *Memories can be personal prisons for us, especially as children.*

Replay

One way in which negative memories affect us is through repetition. When something awful occurs, our brain has a way of staying stuck in that moment and replaying the event over and over again almost like a broken record. Many of us may wonder if there is something we could have done differently, how this could have happened; we replay the event consistently in our minds until it begins to affect our day to day lives especially in most cases our psychiatric state. Studies have shown that long term stress (a result of constant negative thought patterns) has a greater correlation to psychiatric related illness than physical ones. That is to say, negative replay of memories can affect your body but it does a far worse job to your brain and mental state.

How trauma works

I once prayed for a young lady in Ireland who suffered from, let's say, an inability to access her emotions. As I prayed for her I heard the word rape in my spirit. Of course, being careful not to alarm her and treading carefully in case I had heard wrong, I asked her what the worst thing she had ever endured was. She mentioned not being sure if she had been touched as a child but had always lived with a feeling she may have been. I confirmed her suspicion with the word that I had received.

Did you know it's possible to have some parts of your memory repressed as a result of trauma? That is something so traumatic or unbelievable to you that your brain doesn't get rid of the memory but actually *hides* it from you. Psychologists call this repressed memory. Though the mind can't fathom it, it remains in the long-term memory of the individual but is removed from the conscious mind.

Though the brain hides the memory, however, studies show the effects of the memory will still show up in the person's personality or social skills. For example, one of the traits of a person having suffered rape as a child is an inability to be socially free and intimate with others. Though the young lady in my example failed to remember what she suspects may have happened to her as a child, the fruit of such a violation was showing up strongly in her everyday interactions with people.

The job of the Holy Ghost

> "He revealeth the deep and secret things: he knoweth what is in the darkness, and the light dwelleth with him" (Daniel 2: 22)

Daniel describes God as the one who knows the deep and secret things, He knows what's in the dark and light dwells within Him. That is to say, God is able to reveal the things which we do not know. I believe the person of the Trinity to take on this role would be the Holy Ghost. Jesus describes Him in John 14:26 as *"the Comforter, <u>which is</u> the Holy Ghost, whom the Father will send in my name, he shall teach you all things, and bring all things to your remembrance, whatsoever I have said unto you."* The Holy Ghost is able to help you to remember.

> The Holy Ghost is able to help you to remember.

"Why would I want to remember negative events?"

A good and plausible question. It would appear a positive thing for the brain to hide negative events from us, the question would be, if it's so negative, why would I want to remember it? However, repressed memory is possibly one of the most frightening things we can endure. For a person to feel that they cannot remember a segment of their life, have a feeling that part of their memory is not accessible to them or that something may have occurred which they cannot remember, can be likened to a puzzle having a gaping hole in the middle of it or key pieces missing. The picture of one's life is often not complete until one is able to recollect all parts of their life, both the good and the bad.

I do believe, however, that the Lord can use repressed memory for our good if He so wills. For example, in my anecdote above, the young lady may have been unable to emotionally handle the effects of such a revelation previously, repressed memory could have been to her benefit here. However, our God is able to bring things to our memory at the correct time that He is certain we are able to deal with and process such a memory.

When a memory affects day to day life

Some of us have dealt with such negative memories that they affect our day to day life. I have a friend who was sexually abused by a man who held a resemblance to our mentor. Though she loved and absolutely cherished our mentor, there were times that she would freeze up when she saw him because he reminded her of the man that had violated her. I also met with a woman once who had been involved in prostitution. When she eventually met a man that she loved, she couldn't shake the images of her past and the sexual abuse that she endured as a child. When her and this new man in her life would be intimate she would constantly have visions of her past; her memories were stopping her from moving forward in life.

For some of us our memories may not affect us to this depth, though thoughts of the past do play themselves out in how we live, how we relate with our spouse and how we interact with our children. Memories can be the biggest barrier to a successful and thriving life full of joy and peace. It is impossible for one's life to be joyful if one's mind is plagued with guilt, fear, trauma, images or unwanted sounds and words from the past.

The world's remedy

Memories can be so tormenting that we physically desire to run away from them. Some people have sold their homes, sold certain property and even moved countries in a bid to get away from the memories. Some marriages have failed because spouses couldn't overcome the memories of what was said or what was done. In more severe cases some people have sadly taken their own lives when the influx of negative thoughts due to unwanted memories became far too much to bare. Others result to the old age, "pretend it didn't happen", in a bid to fight against the memory that attempts to plague their day to day life.

> *Memories can be so tormenting that we physically desire to run away from them.*

The church's remedy

Following biblical teaching, we know the power of forgiveness in place of bitterness and the harbouring of negative emotions. This can of course guide us on the course of releasing negative memories. However, I have heard many say, *"I have forgiven, but it still affects me"*. What they of course mean to say is, *"though I have chosen to forgive by releasing a prayer and uttering words of positive confession, I cannot shake the memories of the past or rid myself of the feelings and emotions"*. That means, though many of us forgive the individual or situation that occurred, we still find that we suffer the effects in our minds every so often. So, how does one rid themselves of dysfunction when stored memories are at the root?

God's remedy

Well, the truth is that we cannot erase a memory and pretend that something didn't happen, especially that which we remember so strongly. In fact, the more you attempt to rid yourself of a memory the more the mind holds unto the memory and the more it is replayed in our imagination daily. God's remedy is never that we

> God's remedy is never that we pretend that painful moments or traumatic events didn't occur.

pretend that painful moments or traumatic events didn't occur. It is His desire that we sit with Him and talk through our memories. Many of us fail to understand that we are to dialogue our past with the Lord. But this is exactly what David did in the Psalms. David would tell the Lord of how his enemies were out to get him, he would tell the Lord things that He of course (in His omniscience) already knew. Why did David tell God things that He already knew? Because talking through our past is a tool to freedom. For many of us, we keep in situations that have occurred in our lives and never utter the words of our pain or trauma to another soul, a habit of not only dysfunction but ultimate destruction. The mind can only store so much memory of pain, guilt or trauma until it reaches the point of illness or damage, hence the terms, mental health or mental illness.

> *Talking through our past is a tool to freedom.*

Allow the Lord to replace your memories

I have found that the Lord doesn't erase our memories as that would be to take away a piece of our mind's puzzle and leave us empty in an area. However, what the Lord does do is invite us in to *exchange* our memory. He gives us better puzzle pieces than the one we previously had, ultimately creating a much more beautiful picture than the one we had before.

> *And God shall wipe away all tears from their eyes; and there shall be no more death, neither sorrow, nor crying, neither shall there be any more pain: for the former things are passed away. (Revelation 21:4)*

> *Fear not; for thou shalt not be ashamed: neither be thou confounded; for thou shalt not be put to shame: for thou shalt forget the shame of thy youth, and shalt not remember the reproach of thy widowhood any more. (Isaiah 54:4)*

Though I knew the Lord was able to replace our memory with new memories using the same scenario or event in question, I struggled to articulate how He may do so. This wasn't until I had the honour of sharing parts of this book at a young women's gathering in London and had a lady very beautifully share her understanding of what I had just shared on memories. She described God's ability to replace our memories in the following manner…

> *"It's as though when we think back over our life we are watching a silent movie, much of the silent movie is our*

memories of negative, sad or traumatic moments. But when God replaces our memories, He adds His voice to the movie and begins to narrate, "yes you went through this, but this is the moment where I saved you, yes you endured this, but this was necessary for this to take place."

As she shared, I received the revelation: God heals our memory by exchanging our perspective for His. What you saw as the end, God can show you to have been the very beginning; what you imagined as a traumatic life, God can narrate as a story of deliverance of victory to help save and deliver many others. What I saw as traumatic events in childhood, God has used as seeds being sown for the one-day book that I would write on dysfunction. Now when I look back at the same incident that would have brought me fear, pain or shame, I see seed, purpose and deliverance; God has truly exchanged my memory for His.

> *God heals our memory by exchanging our perspective for His.*

The incredible Dr Caroline Leaf explains how doctors once believed the brain to be unchangeable. However, it has since been proven that the brain has neuroplasticity (the ability to adjust itself in response to new situations or environments). This confirms Paul's saying in Romans 12:2 that we be *"transformed by the renewing of our mind"*. Neuroplasticity suggests that the mind can change the brain when it consistently gives it new information, a suggested 63 days for a new memory to be formed.

Should you believe that your memories are buried so deep within you that they will continue to cause dysfunction in your day to day behaviour or choices, think again! You can change your mind by exchanging your memory. Exchange your perspective today for God's perspective. Do what David did in the midst of a deep depression and pull out a pen and paper, divulging your memories unto the Lord and allowing Him to give you His perspective, let Him speak over your silent movie of memories, let Him be your voiceover.

> You can change your mind by exchanging your memory.

> *"...to give unto them beauty for ashes, the oil of joy for mourning, the garment of praise for the spirit of heaviness; that they might be called trees of righteousness, the planting of the* LORD*, that he might be glorified."* (Isaiah 61:3, Extracted)

9

THE CURSE OF KING JECONIAH

Satan the legalist

Did you know that if Satan had a degree it would be first class honours from the highest universities in the world such as Cambridge or Harvard. His subject? Law! He is a skilled and highly competent legalist with the ability to find loop holes and entry ways that even mice would find impossible to squeeze through. If there is any form of open door or unsealed hole you can believe lawyer barrister extraordinaire Satan (LLB) will find it. He's the student that stays up all night researching, he lives in the library reading extra material and finds precedent in your blood line or generational pattern to legally inflict upon you that which he desires. He has staff that work for him and even some human bodies employed as agents on earth have given themselves over to his reign and mastery to act as his workforce. His aim? To steal, kill and destroy everything that the Lord Jesus ever called you to do, have or enjoy on this earth. He aims to destroy not just individuals and callings but family homes, generations, communities and nations. Satan thrives off chaos and feels at home in dysfunction. His resting place is in your hell on earth and he finds ways to keep you in your own personal hell through the things that you don't even know that may be destroying you.

I once heard of an ongoing situation of a violently abusive and promiscuous husband. In this particular instance of his attack, the safety of his wife was paramount; however, she refused to find safety and instead felt the entire thing was her fault. With her mother living not too far away, some 10 minutes from the family home, I believed her mother would step in and convince her daughter to safety. This was not the case. Now, from what I know of parents it would be impossible for any mother to allow their child to endure such physical pain and hardship in a marriage, unless of course she had also endured and remained in the same. And that is exactly what had happened here. The mother's marriage to the father had been the exact same mirroring. A marriage full of violence and promiscuity in which the mother firmly remained, it was no surprise she would feel no sense of urgency to have her daughter leave a potentially life-threatening situation immediately for some time of refuge. This level of violence and disrespect in marriages was clearly a generational pattern that would need to be broken.

When dealing with curses, we must understand how Satan likes to operate. Should we begin to deal with a curse, its effects, the source and the breaking thereof, we must look into why the enemy would desire to set up home within generations. I look at it this way. Satan requires an open door in order to have his way with the world and attempt to disrupt the Lord's plan. To sit within generations is an easy open door. If Satan lays a claim on a particular family, over time through the old and new members of that family, he can ensure he has influence on generations through those individuals. Let's look at a biblical example...

Demons and houses

The house of David was one in which the spirit of lust encamped throughout generations. Starting with David, lust gripped his heart to the degree of it affecting his kingship, the very position he was preordained to stand in even as a young boy. I can hardly believe our young hero that slew the giant Goliath grew into the same man that had another man killed on the battlefield in order to gain his wife. Whether he knew it or not, David was fighting household demons of lust, the same lustful spirit that would go on to affect his son, Solomon, who had countless women at his beck and call. Such a familiar spirit of lust must be one of a generational stronghold. Though we don't know much about David's mother, we can assume through Psalm 51 that David's entry into the world was plagued with sin.

> *Behold, I was shapen in iniquity; and in sin did my mother conceive me. (Psalm 51:5)*

David begins Psalm 51 asking the Lord to have mercy on him. He continues the psalm reminding the Lord of his sorrowful state; he had been shapen in *iniquity* and conceived in *sin*. I would have assumed iniquity and sin to be of the same meaning; however, David makes mention of both being present in his introduction into the world. We can take iniquity to be the hearts permanent state of evil doing, and sin (for David's statement) to be a particular wrong doing. David mentions that he was conceived in sin (a onetime event of wrong doing). From our knowledge of 1 Chronicles 2:13-16 we know that David had two sisters whose father some scholars claim was not Jesse (David's father), but Ammonite King, Nahash (2 Samuel 17:25). Can we assume David's mother played the field and conceived David with Jesse whilst still being with King Nahash or perhaps whilst not yet married to Jesse? I suspect that would be a fair assumption considering

David's plea of being *conceived* in sin. It would also shed light as to why David's brothers (Jesse's sons) regarded David as the little shepherd boy.

> *I was cast upon thee from the womb: thou art my God from my mother's belly. (Psalm 22:10)*

Psalm 22 speaks of the rejection David experienced from his parents. He wasn't lovingly handed over to or dedicated to the Lord, the young shepherd boy was *cast* unto the Lord from the womb.

> *Cast – to throw, dash, forcefully fling something in a particular direction* [5]

If the spirit of lust wasn't inherited by David through Jesse or his mother (which we can fairly assume may have been the case), David certainly experienced enough rejection from his parents, in particular his father Jesse who didn't even consider him worthy of being brought out to prophet Samuel when his household was noted as the place from which the Lord's anointed would be found (1 Samuel 16). The spirit of rejection alone would have acted as a great door opener to usher in the spirit of lust in David's life.

---

[5] https://www.google.co.uk/search?q=cast+definition&oq=cast+definition&aqs=chrome..69i57.9550j0j4&sourceid=chrome&ie=UTF-8

Lust plagued David so much so to the point of death.

Pointer: Spirits such as rejection can cause us to seek love from other sources. Rejection is often a door opener for the spirit of lust. It is no surprise pornography has become a source of false comfort for many in our world today.

> *Rejection is often a door opener for the spirit of lust.*

> *Now king David was old and stricken in years; and they covered him with clothes, but he gat no heat. Wherefore his servants said unto him, Let there be sought for my lord the king a young virgin: and let her stand before the king, and let her cherish him, and let her lie in thy bosom, that my lord the king may get heat. So they sought for a fair damsel throughout all the coasts of Israel, and found Abishag a Shunammite, and brought her to the king. And the damsel was very fair, and cherished the king, and ministered to him: but the king knew her not. (1 kings 1:1-4)*

David's lust problem was so great that his servants were assured the only thing to lift him out of his death bed would be a young virgin and the thought of or promise of sexual pleasure. Having gained entry into the house of David, the spirit of lust was of course transferred to his son Solomon.

> *But king Solomon loved many strange women, together with the daughter of Pharaoh, women of the Moabites, Ammonites, Edomites, Zidonians, and Hittites: Of the nations concerning which the LORD said unto the children of Israel, Ye shall not go in to them, neither shall they come in unto you: for surely they will turn away your heart after their gods: Solomon clave unto these in love. And he had seven hundred wives, princesses, and three hundred concubines: and his wives turned away his heart. For it came to pass, when Solomon was old, that his wives turned away his heart after other gods: and his heart was not perfect with the LORD his God, as was the heart of David his father. For Solomon went after Ashtoreth the goddess of the Zidonians, and after Milcom the abomination of the Ammonites. And Solomon did evil in the sight of the LORD, and went not fully after the LORD, as did David his father.*

(1 Kings 11:1-6)

I wonder if you're as astounded as I am. Can you see the spirit of lust becoming empowered throughout the generations? David sure did have many women, but Solomon could have literally created his own nation of people from the number of wives, princesses and concubines that he held in his time. Solomon's son Rehoboam went on to take the throne, also having wives and concubines as his mere possession.

Now, it's important to remember that Satan's agenda was not simply to infect the Davidic bloodline with lust, he strategically used lust as a means to taint the kings heart away from God.

> *For it came to pass, when Solomon was old, that his wives turned away his heart after other gods: and his heart was not perfect with the LORD his God, as was the heart of David his father. (1 Kings 11:4)*

King David compared with King Saul

Though we all know King Saul as the evil king fuelled with jealousy against his faithful servant and soon to be King David, it is interesting to note that Saul in all his wicked scheming against David and his bad doings as king, did not struggle with the lust problem that David and his household battled.

1 Samuel 14:50 lets us know that Saul's wife's name was Ahinoam. In 2 Samuel 3:7 we are introduced to his concubine Rizpah; however, aside from this there are no further listings of Saul's accounts with strange women, wives in its plural sense or concubines. Saul though a bad king seemed a pretty good (good in comparison to the kings of the time of course) husband and father, especially when looking at his relationship with his son Jonathan. David on the other hand, though a man after God's own heart (1 Samuel 13:14) was plagued with lust and his generations to follow. I call this proof of David's battles being much greater than what appeared to the eye. Could David have been fighting generational demons?

Identifying a curse

I sat with one of my mentees who had travelled down to London to see me. As she sat at the kitchen breakfast bar, I was a few metres away at the sink clearing up the dishes. Suddenly I had a strong feeling (strong enough to gain my attention) of her older sister (who I don't know personally) passing away. I proceeded to ask her if she had a fear of anyone in her family passing away; she replied, "my sister".

In this season of me writing this book, I have found the Lord using the tools of the unknotting to highlight issues in the lives of those around me. I wondered if this was the same situation. Pressing and treading carefully I asked some questions. We got talking and found that her grandmother had passed away under the age of 35, leaving her uncle to raise her own mother. Her own mother had passed away under the age of 35, leaving her older sister to raise *her*. There was clearly a pattern of women having children but not living past the age of 35 to raise their own children, forcing them to be raised by siblings. There was a curse of early death in the female bloodline. By acknowledging it and praying against this, I believe we were able to stand against this curse and call it broken.

When dealing with generational curses the first thing to do is to look for a pattern. Generational curses are made clear through negative patterns of behaviour or a series of demonic similarities through generations. They may run downwards through one or two generations (for example grandmother to mother and then yourself) or they may span across siblings or cousins (yourself, brother and your sister or yourself and cousins).

One such pattern that I noticed in my family in recent times was a curse of broken marriages. I spotted that my grandmother (a mother of five) who herself has been married to my grandfather for many years has children that go on to marry and have children but those marriages for one reason or another, fail to last. For the grandchildren or the nieces that have come out of her side of the family, zero marriages have taken place bar one. If there are 15 grandchildren or nieces and nephews of hers between ages 28 to 40, not one of them have entered into a marital home. Such a pattern severely indicates a generational curse of singleness or broken homes. I wasn't aware of this curse that trailed the family until I turned 27 and the Lord began to alert me to this. I looked around and found that not one of the many females around me in family were married and only once had we ever celebrated an intimate family wedding. I desired marriage in the godly sense of the word and wanted what the Lord had for me in form of my own family home and children, but found myself wondering if this pattern that I had spotted in my family had anything to do with my own singleness. Now, I am not one for curse blaming and will be the first to tell you that the Lord has taken His time in introducing me to my life partner because He had a lot of fixing and mending to do in me; however, that doesn't negate this pattern that I was directly under simply by virtue of being from the family bloodline where such a curse was in operation.

Where do curses come from?

Words of our mouths

> *Death and life are in the power of the tongue, and those who love it will eat its fruit. (Proverbs 18:21)*

I know of a man whose children give him a great amount of grief. Whether it be moments of violence in the home or moments of incredible disrespect. The man, a praying father, has nothing to rely on for change but early morning wake-up calls to ask that the Lord would be the keeper of his home. After hearing one night of severe chaos in the home, I asked the Lord what on earth was going on here, there is no peace in that home, the Lord replied, *"Kike this is the effects of a curse in operation"*. I was astonished.

I asked a woman who grew up with the man some questions and what we found next may shock you. I was told of times in their childhood where this particular now soft-spoken man would act as the tyrant of the home back in Nigeria. During beautifully laid out family breakfast mornings he would overthrow tables of food and cause absolute chaos in the home to his siblings and parents. In his father's hurt over his behaviour he would say, *"your children will do so much worse to you in your own home"*. Chilling words that are still bearing fruit today. His own father had (unknowingly) cursed him and generations to come out of his own mouth. Sure enough in this man's own home, over 30 years later, his own children are indeed doing so much worse to him. Although over 30 years ago, those words are still operating in the spirit realm and are bearing diabolical fruit.

Time empowers a curse

One thing that I have come to learn is that curses don't fizzle out over time, in fact the effects of them get stronger as generations are birthed. Satan is indeed a generational squatter and until someone in the blood line comes in the authority of Christ to kick him out he will remain where he has claimed as his home.

> *When an impure spirit comes out of a person, it goes through arid places seeking rest and does not find it. Then it says, 'I will return to the house I left.' When it arrives, it finds the house unoccupied, swept clean and put in order. (Matthew 12:43-44, NIV)*

We can learn a lot from this example given by Jesus in the book of Matthew. Firstly, we learn that demonic spirits claim human beings as their own home. We also learn that they have a memory, the scripture points out that it remembers the "home" from which it came. We see here that demonic spirits have the ability to travel, "I will return", "when it arrives". Demonic spirits have a destination in mind, they know exactly where they are headed. They are not bound by countries, space or time zones.

This ability to remember, to travel, to have a will and lay claim on a "home" allows demonic spirits to travel and reside in generations. What was on your mother or father can be inflicted upon you, what was on your great grandmother could still be affecting you today without your knowledge.

Curses – a result of evil doing?

Another source of curses are curses that our generations or ancestors have brought upon themselves as a direct result of their idol worship, witchcraft, incest or an overall sinful nature. When we look in the Old Testament we see that mankind often brought curses upon themselves by their very own actions. Idol worship or dedication of future generations to idols, often act as an entry point for generational demonic activity.

Does being a Christian break the curse automatically?

The clear answer to this is, no. But what about 2

Corinthians 5:17-19 I hear you ponder? Paul tells us that:

> *"If anyone be in Christ he is a new creation, the old has gone and the new has come" (extracted).*

You see, I believe Paul's words deal with our ability to let go of our past in order to come into alignment with the truth of Christ's sacrifice on the cross and align with the truth that our spirit man has been made new. He indicates *a new life* in the spirit. But we must remember that though our spirit man be renewed, our soul (where our mind, will and emotions reside) still needs renewing. It is often in our way of thinking, our emotions and our decisions and actions that we find generational patterns.

> *Being a Christian does not negate you from being under a generational curse, what it does is give you the authority to reverse and break every curse and call fourth the blessing of God over your future generations.*

I, like you, would love to believe that once we give our lives over to the Lord and begin to follow Him, or do the works of the ministry, or even become ordained ministers for the edifying of His body, all curses and the like are broken off us, but I fear such an answer would only leave you in further bondage. Unfortunately, I have seen far too many Christians (great Bible believing ones) continue to live under curses and generational patterns. Therefore, what I have concluded is this; being a Christian does not negate you from being under a generational curse, what it does is give you the *authority* to reverse and break every curse and call fourth the blessing of God over your future generations. However, should you fail to exercise that authority, you will unfortunately continue to live under the curse, if one is in operation. Freedom is available to us in Christ, continue to read on.

Breaking a curse

In order to stand in the gap for our families and break a curse, we must do a few things. The first is to of course identify a curse. The second is just as important as the first and it is to believe that curses can be broken. Without faith, we will never see mountains shift and generational curses will continue to plague our households. The third is to admit and repent of our wrong doings or words that may have been spoken, idols that may have been bowed down to or erected (standing in the gap of generations before us), and we must then speak the words of the Lord and the truth of Christ Jesus over that particular situation.

Can curses really be broken?

I would like to take a look at Joseph the father (legal guardian if you would) of Jesus Christ. Did you know that Joseph was under a generational curse?

1 chronicles 3:16 lists a king named, Jeconiah (said to be referred to in other parts of scripture as Coniah, Jeconias or Jehoaichin). In Jeremiah 22:24, though uncertain of what exactly King Jeconiah did during his reign of Judah, this was prophesised concerning him:

> *As I live, saith the LORD, though Coniah the son of Jehoiakim king of Judah were the signet upon my right hand, yet would I pluck thee thence; And I will give thee into the hand of them that seek thy life, and into the hand of them whose face thou fearest, even into the hand of Nebuchadrezzar king of Babylon, and into the hand of the Chaldeans. And I will cast thee out, and thy mother that bare thee, into another country, where ye were not born; and there shall ye die. But to the land whereunto they desire to return, thither shall they not return.*
>
> *Is this man Coniah a despised broken idol? is he a vessel wherein is*

> *no pleasure? wherefore are they cast out, he and his seed, and are cast into a land which they know not? O earth, earth, earth, hear the word of the LORD.*
>
> *Thus saith the LORD, Write ye this man childless, a man that shall not prosper in his days: for no man of his seed shall prosper, sitting upon the throne of David, and ruling any more in Judah. (Jeremiah 22:24-30)*

Wow! You sure wouldn't want to be Jeconiah! Through the prophet Jeremiah it was said of the Lord that Jeconiah would be considered as a childless man, he would not prosper, none of his seed shall prosper and none of them would sit on the throne of David, none of his seed would rule anymore in Judah. Jeconiah was a cursed man and his seed would live under this curse. How shocking it is then to find Jeconiah in Matthew 1:12 listed in the bloodline of Joseph.

> *And after they were brought to Babylon, Jechonias begat Salathiel; and Salathiel begat Zorobabel; (Matthew 1:12)*
>
> *And Jacob begat Joseph the husband of Mary, of whom was born Jesus, who*

is called Christ. (Matthew 1:16)

Joseph, the same man cursed by reason of his association with Jeconiah as prophesised by the prophet Jeremiah, is the same man who would be chosen by the Lord to be known as the earthly father of Jesus. You see, it wasn't just Mary that had found favour with the Lord, Joseph's lineage was clearly receiving the mercy of the Lord.

Though it was said of Joseph's bloodline because of Jeconiah that no seed of theirs would take up the throne of David, Christ (son of Joseph, lineage of Jeconiah) came and not only took, but is promised to sit upon the throne of David. Though it was said that no seed would rule in Judah, Christ Jesus (son of Joseph, lineage of Jeconiah) remains the lion of the tribe of Judah. What an astonishing account of generational redemption! When Jesus came in the picture, when He stepped into a generational curse, He turned that lineage into a generational blessing. Christ Jesus broke the curse of King Jeconiah. Christ Jesus alone is the ultimate curse breaker.

> *When Jesus came in the picture, when He stepped into a generational curse, He turned that lineage into a generational blessing.*

If you are wondering what curse lies in your generational bloodline, what patterns you have studied and seen that indicate the happenings of a curse, be not alarmed, simply invite in Christ. By reason of your adoption into the family of Christ, you now stand with the ability to call upon His name, introduce Christ into the mix, and just like Joseph, watch as generational curses become generational blessings.

With patterns of curses exposed and the truth revealed, barren generations can hear the sounds of children laughing, those experiencing early death can live long and see their children's children, polygamist homes can honour the sanctity of marriage and the poor can live in the bountiful. With Christ, curses can be broken. Open your mouth, call out the curses and patterns that you see, repent, declare the truth of Christ Jesus as the curse breaker, speak what the word says over that particular thing by finding scripture to support your argument and watch curses break at the authority of His name.

10

CREATING NEW LEGACIES

What a packed and heavy nine chapters that you've just read through. I suppose you can call the previous chapter's diagnosis, a thorough examination as to the roots of dysfunction, helping you to identify where some of your issues may have come from. You'll have noticed that much of this book has not been healing tools but rather a walkthrough of where damage or knots may have occurred. Much of the healing that we require is simply by coming to the realisation of where the damage initially occurred; however, it is my prayer to now help you to know how to create new legacies going forward.

Looking at brokenness in our past generations

and family line can be heart-breaking. I am sure that as you've read through this book you have felt or remembered deeper levels of dysfunction that you never knew existed. Maybe you remembered new instances or happenings or spotted new patterns and possibly felt yourself feeling angry, frustrated or hurt by the way you were raised or the dysfunction you were brought up in. I pray you'll consider the points made below…

Consider the role of the enemy

When creating new legacies it is imperative that you keep in mind the role of the enemy. As a predator seeking whom he may devour, he often finds children that have come from broken homes as easy prey. Often finding places where pain and hurt or trauma lie, he seeks the root of pain not to ease the discomfort but to increase the severity and cause further damage. If you fail to see the hand of the enemy in your family and generational dysfunction, you will consistently (and wrongly) see those that you believe have failed you and will end up bitter and full of regret. Regret that you were not born into a more functioning normal, regret that life dealt you some harsh blows and regret that you were affected by some things which truly were no fault of your own.

Double victims

For many of us we may feel it is a parent or both parents that let us down or didn't raise us appropriately. However, I ask you to consider this; they did the best they could with what they knew. I heard a story once of a woman whose mother sold her to a man for sexual favours. A mother sold her daughters virginity for probably no more than £50 in British currency. She sounds like the worst mother on earth, right? Not until you hear about the grandmother. The grandmother held a prostitution ring at her home and the mother I speak of was in fact victim of her own mother's trade. Suddenly she becomes the victim now, doesn't she?

> *Consider that the perpetrator was first the victim.*

For many of us having walked through broken generations, it would be a lack of wisdom to fail to consider that the perpetrator was first the victim. We have all heard the term, "hurt people, hurt people", this is true. When victims of generational patterns become parents themselves they often parent out of the information that they have been given and not out of the truth of the word of God or even mere human moral compass. Could your parent have parented out of their dysfunction and given only what they knew to give? Sure, they could have gained further knowledge, sure they could have learnt better, sure the mother in my example could have kicked in some level of human and motherly decency not to sell her own child; however, brokenness can at times know no bounds and dysfunction often breeds dysfunction.

Go back and deal...

In creating new legacies, I encourage you to firstly go back and deal with that which you have identified as dysfunctional by simply talking. Talking through the things that you have identified or learnt in this book with those in your family, siblings, parents or grandparents, if you're permitted the opportunity, will bring true liberation. If circumstances or dysfunction so far gone means that talking is currently not an option, then prayer acts, not as an alternative, but an ever-present consistent safe haven. Praying through the issues that you have identified, the patterns that you have spotted and the dysfunctional moments or foundations that have affected you, allows the Lord to step in and bring healing.

Mercy over judgement

In the legal system, we examine criminal law by looking at two things known in the Latin as 'Actus Reus' (guilty act) and 'mens rea' (guilty mind). This is to say, if a person were to walk out of a store having placed items they had yet to pay for in their bag and were caught by the stores security, there are two things that must be considered for their conviction. The actus Reus is often easy to determine, did they do it? That's often a simple, yes or no. It's the mens rea, the guilty mind, which can take juries and court systems a while to determine. In determining the mens rea, the courts go as far as to consider mitigating circumstances such as that of limited liability. That is, yes, this person committed the crime, but is there any reasonable reason to be considered that makes them *not* guilty? Were they suffering from a mental illness, were they under the duress of another etc. In essence, the legal system exercises mercy before applying judgement. When it comes to those that have done us a wrong or failed to nurture us as they should have, we can apply this same principle; yes, the individual or family structure may have failed in their role or duty, but why? What was their own background, did they do the best that they could with the knowledge that they had?

The gift of adoption

> *For ye have not received the spirit of bondage again to fear; but ye have received the Spirit of adoption, whereby we cry, Abba, Father.* (Romans 8:15)

What a beautiful promise. Where earthly families fail, the Lord promises to adopt us into His own family. Knowing that our family units would lack the complete resources to provide sustenance and fuel for our wholeness, the Lord declares Himself as our Abba Father. The word Abba translates in the Greek to mean "source". The Lord is declaring here that He Himself will become our origin. We, along with our families, can make the decision to leave old legacies and tainted pasts behind and reach for the outpouring of Heaven's resources and claim a new surname. A spirit of adoption is not a haughty one that says, *"I do away with my family, they are no good"*, it is one which thankfully utters, *"when I had no place to turn, when what my lineage and I knew to do failed, He stretched out His hands and said come, I'll take you in"* what a picture of grace.

Christ makes the difference

A great comforter for me is the above statement, Christ makes the difference! Whether you feel you were raised in dysfunction, raised in normality or not raised at all; Christ makes the difference! I envision it like this, whether a bottle almost full of water or one almost empty, both require *more* in order to be considered full. Christ is the more that we all need. You are not behind or lacking because of your background or lineage, not when you allow Christ to make the difference. Truly allowing Him to unknot you of the issues that have attempted to plague you will transfer you from a place of dysfunction to functional. Just ask Gomer the prostitute or David the Shepherd boy. Even still, ask Joseph or Esther or poor little abandoned Moses. All are examples of some form of childhood dysfunction, yet when they allowed the fatherhood and power of God into their life, they went from outcast to main characters in God's very own story book. God does incredible work with the seemingly dysfunctional.

> *Whether a bottle almost full of water or one almost empty, both require more in order to be considered full. Christ is the more that we all need.*

Stand in the gap

There must be one that is willing to stand in the gap for a lineage or a generation in order to begin change. In my place of prayer, rising early or sleeping late, I have bound, loosed, declared and proclaimed over not only myself, but my generation, my parents, my grandparents, tearing down idols, casting down imaginations, declaring truth and calling forth salvation. You can do the same. In fact, I am certain the Lord is waiting on you to do the same. If you have siblings who see what you see, why not agree together and stand in the gap? If you stand alone, then know that you are never alone, there is one that is mighty that intercedes for you as you stand in the gap.

God cares about your lineage

Oh, how He cares! We must not fall for the enemy's lie that God wants to deliver us and us alone. Our God takes delight in seeing families restored and homes set free. Yes, your family has been a victim of Satan's mass attack on the family unit, but our God delights in restoring dead marriages, returning stray children home and mending broken sibling relationships. It is His great delight to see the family unit be all that He intended it to be; fruitful, having dominion and multiplying right here on earth! Whatever your current situation, believe that God not only cares to heal it, but that He is waiting on your prayers so that He can begin to move and do the miraculous.

Prayer

Father,

I thank You for Your great love. Your love that covers and saturates the family members of every hand that holds this book. I plead the blood of Jesus that washes clean and makes whole over every family. I command a healing and restorative anointing over every broken *home, every broken mind and every broken heart as a result of hurting and fractured families. Bring together fathers and sons Lord, mend the heart of mothers, heal wounded children from the pains of their childhood God, and deliver the oppressed that are still tied to memories from their family home. Send out an anointing that proclaims liberty to the bound father, restore the lost and stolen years. For every father and mother estranged from their children I pray a returning home, I command phone calls of restoration and forgiveness to be made, hugs to be had and tears to be shed in love and in the joy of unity. Lord, I thank You that the family was your idea, it's Your precious institution, enter in Holy Ghost and do a work in households. Send stray children home, untangle Your sons and daughters from curses and patterns of old. Oh, I ask that You expose Lord God, expose Satan and his crafty works. Shine, shed and blast a light on the cracks of where the enemy cowardly hides himself in generations. Move as You would to begin to heal Lord. Lay Your hand on a representative in the family unit to begin to hear Your voice and know Your will concerning their particular household.*

And I praise you that You are simultaneously building new legacies for their lineage to come. I thank You for those in new families and now raising their own children that the chains of old would stop with them and goes no further. I thank You that broken marriages be no more, poverty, early death and fear loose their grip. I thank You that through Your wisdom and knowledge we know what to do in order to break free. Thank You Jesus for the unknotting of our souls from dysfunction!

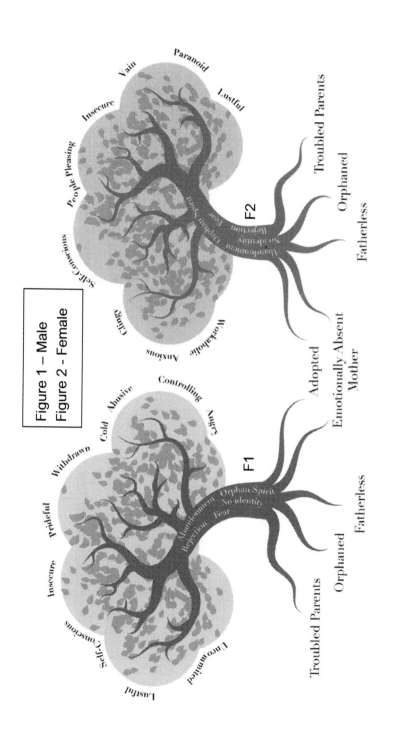

OTHER TITLES BY THE AUTHOR

The Delivery Room:
Discovering the real me in Him

Intimacy:
Finding life in the secret place

CONTACT THE AUTHOR

Via **www.theunknottingbook.com**

Via the author's publishing house, LoveChild Publishing:
lovechildpublishing@hotmail.com

Via social media platforms:
@totallykeeks

NOTES

NOTES

NOTES

NOTES

Made in the USA
San Bernardino, CA
16 July 2018